ALSO BY MAXINE BENEBA CLARKE

Foreign Soil
Carrying the World

Maxine Beneba Clarke

THE HATE RACE

A Memoir

corsair

For my mother

CORSAIR

First published in Australia and New Zealand in 2016 by Hachette Australia
First published in Great Britain in 2017 by Corsair

1 3 5 7 9 10 8 6 4 2

Copyright © Maxine Beneba Clarke 2016

The moral right of the author has been asserted.

Lyrics of 'Jamaica Farewell', written by Irving Burgie,
reproduced on page 115 with permission.

*Pseudonyms have been used in this book and other details altered where
necessary to protect the identity and privacy of people mentioned.*

Text design by Bookhouse, Sydney
All rights reserved.

A CIP catalogue record for this book
is available from the British Library.

ISBN: 978-1-4721-5150-6

Typeset in 12/17.8 pt Bembo by Bookhouse, Sydney

Printed and bound in Great Britain by Clays Ltd, St Ives plc

Papers used by Corsair are from well-managed forests
and other responsible sources.

MIX
Paper from
responsible sources
FSC® C104740
www.fsc.org

Corsair
An imprint of
Little, Brown Book Group
Carmelite House
50 Victoria Embankment
London EC4Y 0DZ

An Hachette UK Company
www.hachette.co.uk

www.littlebrown.co.uk

PROLOGUE

DRIVING SLOWLY ALONG the artery of North Road, you can track the varied and changing demographics of Melbourne's inner east. Palatial beachfront mansions and Art Deco apartments slowly give way to overlarge suburban houses. This is the east side of the city – where everything is two-point-five-kids-and-a-four-wheel-drive respectable, un-grungy all the way from Elwood to Huntingdale.

I'm walking along the short stretch of North Road that takes me from my own street in the white-picket-fence, increasingly gentrified suburb of East Bentleigh to my son's primary school, one of three primary schools within walking distance of our home. I'm bloody tired. In fact, I'm probably looking forward to the school holidays even more than my son. He's five and a half, and in his first year at primary school. For the last ten weeks, the poor little critter's been absolutely *smashed* with tiredness come three-thirty pick-up. He shuffles out of school babbling and incoherent, offering nonsensical insights into various parts of his day: which kid fell over and skinned their knee during snack time, what flavour icy pole he chose at lunchtime with a full analysis of exactly why.

I'm wheeling my chubby five-month-old daughter along in her pram, looking forward to two weeks of pyjama-clad French toast mornings, museum trips and non-school-assigned reading.

'Fuck off, bitch.' The voice comes from behind me.

Exactly what I *don't* need this afternoon is to be caught up in someone's very public domestic.

'Go on, fuck off.'

An uneasy feeling runs down my spine. This isn't some domestic dispute: he's talking to me. I'm unprepared, stop for a second, startled. It's been about ten months since I was openly abused on the street by a total stranger. Since moving from Sydney to Melbourne four years back, it's never happened so close to my home.

The white ute draws level with me, slows down. It's around three and the traffic on North Road is almost bumper to bumper. The car behind the ute slams on its brakes.

'Fuck off, you black bitch,' the ute driver screams from the open window. 'Go on, fuck off. You make me sick, you fucken black slut. Go drown your kid! You should go drown your fucken kid. Fuck off, will you!'

Suddenly, there's that chest-tightening feeling. That heart-in-my-throat, pulse-in-my-temples fear. The dry tongue. The gasping for breath. The nakedness. The remembering how it can happen anywhere, at any time. That can't-think freeze. I am four years old, on my first day of preschool, standing underneath the mulberry tree, watching another little girl's lip curl up with disgust as she stares at me. I am slouched down on the high school bus, head bowed, pretending not to notice the spit-ball barrage, the whispered name-calling.

My baby daughter thinks it's funny. She's chuckling, kicking her fat legs in glee at the loud voice coming from the vehicle. My knuckles are gripping the pram so tightly that the fingertips on my right hand have started to go numb. I look straight ahead, trying not to pick up the pace too much. The turn-off for my son's school is a few hundred metres away. Another horn beeps. It's the motorist behind the ute. I know the ute driver's a young bloke, but I don't want to look any closer. That's part of what he wants.

'Fuck off, blackie! Why don't you just piss off? Bitch! Go the fuck back to where you came from, back to your own fucken country, nigger!' He puts his foot on the accelerator and the ute screeches away.

I round the corner. Off the main road, I stop the pram and sit down on somebody's tan-brick front fence. I can't breathe properly. Tears are streaming down my face. I'm heartbroken, but also angry — not at the young ute driver, at myself. For letting this upset me. I should be used to this. I should know better. I'm also thankful my daughter isn't a few years older, old enough to understand. I'm thankful my five-year-old wasn't walking with me. I'm also thankful the bloke in the ute couldn't see the baby: her beautiful caramel skin, her to-die-for medium brown eyes, the light brown ringlet curls starting to dance their way across her little fat head. I know that this, too, might add fuel to the fire.

I compose myself, check my watch. The school bell rings in five minutes. I have to make up time. The mother of a boy in my son's class falls into step with me.

'How's your day been?'

I'm still shaking, can't answer her for a moment.

'Um. Sorry . . . I'm . . . I'm a little bit uh . . . Sorry. Some guy driving along the street just started yelling at me. I'm feeling a bit out of it, actually . . .'

'Just now? What happened? What did he say?'

'Go back to your own effing country. You know the drill.'

I can tell she doesn't. She's standing there with her mouth gaping open in shock. I feel embarrassed now, ashamed I even brought it up.

'I'm okay. Don't worry about it. It just hasn't happened for a while, that's all.'

She starts to stammer something, then looks away uncomfortably. 'That's horrible,' she offers finally. 'I'm so sorry. I don't know what the hell gets into people. That's just awful. I'm sorry you had to go through that.'

I don't want sympathy. I want to un-hear what I just heard, un-experience what just happened. If racism is a shortcoming of the heart, then experiencing it is an assault on the mind. *You should go drown your fucken kid! Go the fuck back to where you came from, nigger.* The cumulative effect of these incidents is like a poison: it eats away the very essence of your being. Left unchecked, it can drive you to the unthinkable.

It's day five of the school holidays and we've barely left the house. When we do go out, to the shops or park, I can feel all the white people looking at us. I don't want to have to consider what they're probably thinking.

I'm supposed to take my son to a theatre show tomorrow. He's been looking forward to it for over a month: grins widely every time he remembers the upcoming excursion. The kids' theatre show is, quite frankly, my idea of hell. My son knows that, which is why he takes so much pleasure in asking me if I'm excited about it.

'Are you looking forward to the show tomorrow, Mum? I can't wait!'

'I'm so excited about it, I think I'm going to wet my pants,' I respond, deadpan.

'Why do I have to have such a silly mother?' He falls over onto the carpet in hysterics, rolls his eyes.

I do feel like I'm going to wet my pants. It's only been one term, but I don't want my child to go back to school. I remember, my god, so well, the unforgiving playgrounds of my youth.

I don't ever want to go out of our house. We might sit next to somebody who racially abuses us under their breath. The usher who tears the ticket might wipe their hands on their shirt in disgust after their fingers brush mine. The server at the snack bar might spit on our hot chips during interval. Somebody might tell me I should drown my own child.

Go back to your own fucking country.

This is my country, that much I am sure. I was born here, the child of Black British parents, in 1979, in a maternity ward of Sydney's Ryde Hospital, on the stolen land of the Dharug people. My early ancestors were part of the Atlantic slave trade. They were dragged screaming from their homes in West Africa and chained by their necks and ankles, deep in the mouldy hulls of slave ships, destined to become free labour for the New World. If slaves were lucky, they died in transit to the Caribbean – bodies thrown overboard, washed clean of the blood, sweat and faeces in which they'd spent most of the harrowing journey. If they

Maxine Beneba Clarke

survived, they found themselves in a nightmare: put to work on the harshest plantations on earth, overseen by some of the cruellest masters in the history of the Atlantic slave trade. I am the descendant of those unbroken.

I carry proudly the burnished mahogany of my ancestors, though my Africa is four continents, four hundred years of slavery, one forced migration, two voluntary migrations and many lifetimes ago. So long ago, in fact, that Africa herself might not now recognise me. So long ago that when I die, the fierce, fertile continent of my origin might refuse my spirit entry: the wooden pombibele might refuse to drum out my funeral rites. Mwene Puto, the Lord of the Dead, with long thin fingers as blond as bone, might refuse to appear and claim me, and my soul will be spirited south, away from my first motherland, past the open corners of Yemen and Somalia and out into the Indian Ocean, sent packing back to Australia, the land of my birth: *my country* – my *children's* country. The only home we know.

Part One

1.

PHOTOGRAPHS OF THE time show my father in flared cords and tightly fitted shirts, his oval-shaped afro rising high above his head. There's my drama-school-graduate mother, dainty and petite in velour turtlenecks and large wooden earrings, sparkly eyed and beautiful. Both of them are Black Britain to a tee: full to bursting with seventies hippie hopefulness. And my god, their *youth*. Over the years, snippets of the journey, of *how your father and I came to Australia*, have been told and retold. The margins between events have blended and shifted in the *tell* of it. There's that folklore way West Indians have, of weaving a tale: facts just so, gasps and guffaws in all the right places – because, after all, what else is a story for?

There are myriad ways of telling it. The young black wunderkind, the son of a cane-cutter with the god-knew-how-it-happened first-class degree in pure mathematics. Gough Whitlam, the sensible new Australian prime minister, dismantling the last vestiges of the White Australia Policy. That fool English politician Enoch Powell, and his *rivers of blood* anti-immigration nonsense. Two academics arranging to meet at London's Victoria station.

3

A Qantas jumbo jet. My parents' unforgettable arrival in Sydney, at the Man Friday Hotel.

When I gather the threads in my fingers, this is how I'd have it weave.

It's 1973. My father's parents, Louella and Duncan Clarke, gaze across the hall of the local West Indian Club to where their first son holds court among the neighbourhood well-wishers. Louella clenches her eyelids tightly shut, feeling she might well cry with pride. Then, slowly opening her eyes, she grips her husband's worn, tired hand in hers.

'Lou, all de trouble. It wort it. It well wort it, woman.' My grandad turns to his wife, a smile dancing in his bloodshot eyes.

'What trouble ye talkin bout, Dun?' she would have asked, in that cheeky tone she often used to rile him.

Duncan would have looked at Louella then, well shocked. Surely the woman wasn't losing her mind just yet. Surely she hadn't forgotten the battles of these last thirty years. The wretched three-week boat journey from Jamaica. Living in freezing English boarding houses. The riots. The early days with those fascists stirring up the streets so that no black person felt safe walking them day or night.

But then Duncan would have noticed, in the corner of Louella's eye, the twinkle which had first drawn him to her, all those years ago back in Jamaica.

'Ye never had any trouble wid dat chile *yeself*,' Louella would've continued. 'If mi do recall, was mi who, screamin an cussin so loud all-a Kingston musta heard, did squeeze de bwoy outta parts dat surely nat meant fe a likkle head wid a brain in it dat big te pass through!'

Duncan, he'd have laughed then. He'd have let echo one of those deep belly rumbles of his. Louella, she'd've joined him, chuckling away. They'd have sat together – I'm sure of it – side by side, watching the first of their four children celebrate his success.

My father, Bordeaux Mathias Nathanial Clarke, was the first-born son of two Jamaicans, and named with all the pomp and expectation that entailed. Born in the Jamaican capital of Kingston, Bordeaux migrated to London with his parents at nursery school age. At twenty-five, he'd just become one of the first in his community to secure a degree from a British university.

Thirty years since the first wave of mass migration to England from the Caribbean, Black London was finally coming into its own. The anticipation could be felt in the salons, pubs and jerk chicken take-outs of Tottenham, Seven Sisters, Brixton, Birmingham, Walthamstow.

If ever the loyalty of Britain's far-flung Africa-descended subjects left scattered over the West Indian islands post-slavery was in question, the voluntary participation of tens of thousands of young black men and women in the Second World War effort had put paid to these misgivings. By 1945, officially at least, West Indians were seen as 'true' citizens, whose patriotism was no longer open to scrutiny: theirs was an allegiance which had been sworn in blood.

British immigration officers posted throughout the Caribbean to encourage migration to fill post-war employment shortages were very persuasive. My Jamaican paternal grandparents and Guyanese maternal grandparents lined up for passage to build a new life for themselves and their young families in a place where – they were assured – the streets were *paved* with gold.

Black people had lived in England, in sparse numbers, since slavery, but in 1945 the *Empire Windrush* ship pulled into the Tilbury docks carrying over four hundred and fifty Jamaicans. Those on board – mostly men – had braved the same Atlantic Ocean the British had used to forcibly transport their forebears to the plantations some hundred years back. They came brimming with hope; searching for work; thirsting for the better life Britain would surely offer.

So began the slow parade of ships from the islands to the British motherland. At the conclusion of each weeks-long voyage, hundreds of tired, hopeful passengers were unceremoniously dispersed into the grey ports of London. Often ostracised by their neighbours, belittled by their colleagues, short-changed by their employers and extorted by their landlords, the new arrivals moved from boarding house to boarding house, day labour job to day labour job, constantly on the move through the drab outer suburbs of the capital. The new West Indian arrivals desperately searched out their countrymen in the cold, lonely corners of a country which turned out to be nothing like they'd dared to dream.

But here, not thirty years later, Bordeaux Clarke had become living proof of the opportunities afforded by the struggles and sacrifice of his parents' migration. Here was the accomplished young black man every West Indian father wanted their knock-kneed little brown boys to become.

This is how I'd have it sing.

'Ow, Dad. Ow!' Dragged by the ear by his Jamaican father across the room to meet the new graduate, a small black boy pushed his lips out into a stubborn pout and scowled. Bordeaux stifled his amusement and tried to appear a suitably impressive role model for the poor kid.

'See dis man?' the boy's father, a respected neighbourhood elder, asked.

''Course I see im, Dad – 'e's standin right in fronta me!' The boy squirmed out of his father's grasp.

'Chile, ye nyah know what's good fe ye. Show de man some respect or me gwan give ye a lickin!' The man cupped his hand under his ten-year-old's chin, raising the boy's face up towards the statuesque scholar standing in front of them. 'Dis young man somebody ye should aspire te be, bwoy,' he lectured. 'Kiss de man's feet. Go on – bend down right now, an kiss de man feet.'

This is a tale my Grandad Duncan once told me, to demonstrate how much respect my father's education had commanded. That West Indian way, of spinning a tale. Bordeaux, if I know it right, would have shifted uncomfortably from foot to foot, while the serious man pointed down towards his black Dr Marten boots. Bordeaux, he'd have laughed, patting the nervous kid on the shoulder and waving the pair away, the older man still looking respectfully back over his shoulder.

Since the Clarke family's arrival in London from Jamaica some twenty-three years before, it had been *Bordy this* and *Bordy that*.

'Bordy's teacher, dem nyah like im. Dem give de bwoy grief jus cause de chile too gifted.'

'Bordy, im so smart, im really gwan meyk sometin of imself, ye know.'

If they hadn't heard enough praise about the boy from the very proud Louella and Duncan Clarke over the years, all of Tottenham now appeared to have concrete validation of what the couple had been preaching: that their first boy, Bordy, was nothing short of brilliant. That in England, if a black child worked hard enough, any dream was achievable.

Bordy had *paper*. This wasn't just *any* old piece of paper Bordy held, but a PhD from an *English* university. A PhD in not just *any* old subject, but *mathematics*. Tssssk. Any old Montego Bay layabout knew that was a damn hard gig.

To boot, Bordy had also recently married Millie and Robert Critchlow's middle daughter, Cleopatra, the young Guyanese actress who'd recently graduated from the National School of Speech and Drama. A beauty, she was, and Bordy, with his soundwaves and equations and geek-glasses, with his numbers and slightly abrasive manner, he'd somehow nabbed her. God only knew how.

There had always been problems in England for people like Bordy and Cleo. For West Indians, that is. In the summer of 1958, fours years after the arrival of the *Empire Windrush*, random violent attacks on black people on the streets of London escalated over the course of two weeks, culminating in race rioting on the streets of Notting Hill, in West London. Hundreds of white folk – many of them working-class teddy boys spurred on by involvement in fascist anti-immigration groups – stormed the streets, attacking the houses of black immigrants.

Ten years later, in 1968, around the time Bordy and Cleo were thinking about studying for their A levels, the world seemed to be in the midst of a race crisis. In the United States, civil rights leader Martin Luther King was assassinated, leading to widespread race rioting across the country. In South Africa, the movement against the apartheid system of racial segregation had been temporarily stifled by political repression. At home in

London, a politician named Enoch Powell gave a speech at the Conservative Association meeting in Birmingham. Hair slicked back, black jacket tightly buttoned, sparse moustache jumping over thin, pursed lips, he declared:

> 'In this country, in fifteen or twenty years' time, the black man will have the whip hand over the white man' . . . It almost passes belief that at this moment twenty or thirty additional immigrant children are arriving from overseas in Wolverhampton alone every week . . . Those whom the gods wish to destroy, they first make mad. We must be mad, literally mad, as a nation to be permitting the annual inflow . . .

Powell warned of English wives in childbirth turned away from overcrowded hospitals, of white children unable to obtain places in local schools, of neighbourhoods changed beyond recognition. In the general election of 1970, the centre-right Conservative Party of the United Kingdom won an unexpected victory.

Despite these racial tensions, migrants of colour and their British-born children had truly made London their home. In Tottenham, a few island grocery shops had sprung up: aisles stacked with jerk seasoning, tinned ackee, smoked salt fish and bruised plantains. The occasional black hair salon could be seen, with racks of multi-coloured hair-weave pieces, giant tubs of sticky dreadlock wax and netted sleeping caps spilling onto the footpaths. After twenty or so years, a strong black community was being forged.

Following his graduation, Bordeaux was offered a teaching post at Nottingham University. The post-war boom ground to a standstill. The economic climate in England started to falter. The country slid into recession. One of Bordeaux's university colleagues was about to return home to Australia to take up a teaching post. The Australian man's wife got on well with Cleopatra and the two couples had formed a solid friendship. The Australians advised Cleo and Bordy to consider moving to Australia.

'Leave Great Britain,' they urged. 'Jump ship before it sinks.'

Bordy and Cleo knew Australia was a wealthy country colonised by the United Kingdom. They knew that Australia was a nation founded on the genocide, degradation and dispossession of black Indigenous inhabitants. They knew that, for many decades, Australians had lived under the White Australia Policy – which openly preferenced white migrants and excluded migrants of colour. The White Australia Policy was a system that, in 1919, Australian Prime Minister William Morris 'Billy' Hughes hailed as 'the greatest thing we have achieved'. Decades later, after the outbreak of the Second World War, then Australian Prime Minister John Curtin had proclaimed: 'This country shall remain forever the home of the descendants of those people who came here in peace in order to establish in the South Seas an outpost of the British race.'

But the young Australian couple assured Bordy and Cleo that things were changing. The White Australia Policy had been dismantled. The visionary new prime minister, Gough Whitlam, had been elected on a platform of increased immigration and land rights for Indigenous Australians. Excitement was in the air. Change was coming.

———

On their return to Australia, the young couple started posting job openings back to Bordeaux, for positions in New South Wales, where they would be within reach to help the young black couple settle in to their new country.

Months ticked by without news. Upheaval within the Whitlam government had caused a freeze on government job appointments. Cleo and Bordy could make neither head nor tail of the ruckus, but it appeared Gough Whitlam, the man their friends had championed as the mandated architect of the *new Australia*, was no longer the prime minister. The silence suddenly broke, and a reputable university in Sydney's west contacted Bordeaux to let him know they were seriously considering him for a position. He was required to send further identification, including a photograph.

Aware of the lack of diversity in Australia, Bordy strategically declined to include a photograph with his documentation. Weeks later, my father received notification that a professor from the Australian university happened to be visiting London, and would like to meet up with him to discuss the job offer. The two academics decided Victoria station would make a good initial meeting point.

This is how my mother tells it. This is how the story hums.

'How will I know who you are?' the professor asked my father.

'I'll be wearing a pinstriped suit,' Bordy replied carefully, 'and carrying an umbrella.'

'I'll be carrying a red Qantas bag,' the Australian professor said.

The day of the meeting, Bordeaux Clarke, dressed in his pinstriped suit, nervously kissed his young wife goodbye and headed to Victoria station. The train pulled in. Businessmen in dark suits, women pushing prams, groups of teenagers and families with suitcases filled the platform. The black man wearing his best pinstriped suit and carrying a large umbrella greeted the Chinese Australian professor carrying a red Qantas bag.

That folklore way of weaving the tale.

No-one was more surprised than Louella and Duncan Clarke when they found out that their brilliant young son had applied for a position at a university in Australia. As far as anyone knew, Australia was some bottom-of-the-earth island that had banned black folk from coming in for as long as possible, after shooting dead most of the ones they found there in the first place.

News of the newly married couple's impending migration was the talk of black Tottenham.

'Ye hear dat Bordy, Lou an Dun's bwoy, im teykin im new wife Cleopatra to anudda country?' one customer would remark to another down at the West Indian goods shop on the corner of West Green Road.

'Nah, me nyah know dat. Ye serious? Where de two-a dem goin?'

'Dem gwan Austreeyleea.'

'Where dem gwan?'

'Austreeyleea.'

'Austreeyleea? Where de hell dat?'

'Me nat sure. Somewhere at de bottom of de world. It British rule.'

'Black folk dem live down dere?'

'Is anyone guess!'

'Why dem gwan dere?'

'Bordy im get teachin job in de university dere.'

'Me thought im already got teachin job up Nottingham?'

'Well, im own fadda Duncan tell mi dat im leavin de country an goin dere.'

'Lawd! Dat damn shame.'

I can see them now, the gossipmongers, shaking their heads in confusion as the shop attendant rang up their items.

This is how I tell it, or else what's a story for.

2.

IN 1976, AFTER twenty-nine hours of travel, nine cardboard-consistency meals and two sleepless nights, racked with excitement, anxiety and anticipation, Bordeaux and Cleopatra Clarke arrived at Sydney International Airport. They disembarked wide-eyed from the enormous kangaroo-stamped jet, in the company of a hundred other tired travellers.

Their first impression of their new country was the sheer brightness: a luminous southern hemisphere sunlight they had never seen before in an impossibly clear blue sky. It was glorious, that light, as if they'd stepped suddenly out of grey, dreary Kansas into the motion-picture technicolour of Oz. Terra Australis. Endless possibility.

The ride out to Chatswood was longer than Bordy and Cleopatra had anticipated. The sparsely populated suburbs stretched as far as the eye could see. Large square houses stood on enormous blocks of clipped green grass, bordered by picket fences. The driver snuck curious glances at the well-dressed young black couple in his rear-view mirror as he drove to the North Shore address they'd given him.

The car eventually slowed to a halt outside the hotel where the university had booked a room for my parents until more-permanent accommodation could be found. The excited but jet-lagged couple stood in the driveway, looking up at the hotel. Cleopatra shook her head in disbelief, leaned over and checked the number on the hotel letterbox against the address they'd been given. The couple locked eyes, shocked. The sign above the entrance proclaimed: *Man Friday Hotel*. They both knew Man Friday well. Man Friday, the Carib cannibal turned loyal servant of Robinson Crusoe. Man Friday the faithful who, in Defoe's novel, loved his master so fiercely that, after serving the shipwrecked man on the island, he followed Crusoe back to England for a lifetime of willing servitude.

Bordy reassured his wife, as they hauled their suitcases from the back of the vehicle and the taxi slowly pulled out of the driveway. I can hear them now, those bogongs of doubt beginning their dusty-winged beat beneath my mother's rib cage. *What kind of country is this?* Cleo glanced quickly over to the street sign at the end of the road. Help Street it read, the white letters screaming out against the dark background.

Wishing to celebrate their arrival with the obligatory English wine and cheese before finally catching some sleep, Bordeaux and Cleopatra were directed to the local bottle shop by wary hotel management. The man behind the counter immediately directed the young black couple to the cask wine section. Bordeaux and Cleopatra, who had never seen cask wine before, peered through the holes in the cardboard casks to inspect the foil bags which appeared to contain the wine. Not realising they'd been directed towards the cheap, nasty booze assumed to be their consumption of choice, they selected one of the more expensive casks and headed back to the counter.

In the adjoining Franklins supermarket, wooden crates and cardboard boxes were stacked from floor to ceiling, creating makeshift aisles which rendered navigation of their trolley an Olympic feat. Ugly black block-writing screamed the names of smallgoods across white, plastic packages. Cleopatra reached instinctively for one of the few coloured packets in the cheese section of the refrigerator. Bordeaux caught his young wife's hand mid-air, recoiling in shock. In giant blue lettering, the word COON leered at them.

Again, those beasts of doubt, waking and turning, deep in my mother's gut. *What have we done? What have we done?!*

During Cleo and Bordy's week-long stay at the Man Friday Hotel, there was no forgetting the ill-omened name. The distinctive hotel logo danced across pristine white towels, napkins, sheets and curtains: an embroidered trail of tiny black footprints, exploratory smudges on uncharted white territory.

In another sign the fates were stacked against them, the couple who had urged Cleo and Bordy to migrate to Australia made an unexpected move to rural South Australia to take over the family farm. Their time left in New South Wales overlapped just a few months with Bordy and Cleo's arrival, and then the young black couple found themselves well and truly alone.

Eighteen months after their arrival in Australia, my parents settled in the small outer Sydney suburb of Kellyville. Located on the rural fringe, houses in the area were comparatively cheap, and the sleepy suburban village was within commuting distance of my father's teaching job at the university. Then, too, it was the kind of place the young couple envisaged they might start and raise a family.

The suburb was named after Hugh Kelly, who'd arrived in New South Wales as a convict in the early 1800s. On his release, Kelly amassed land in the area along with a pub, the Bird in Hand, which had stood on the intersection of two main roads: Wrights and Windsor. When Kelly died, around 1884, the land of his estate was divided up into farmlets and the area became known as Kellyville. Kellyville had remained semi-rural until the mid-sixties, when roughly a thousand homes were developed in an area that became known as 'the village'.

Kellyville village was a cluster of mostly brick houses in the style of classic seventies suburbia. Three bedrooms. One bathroom. Carport or single garage. Concrete driveway. Carefully edged yard. In summer, lawn sprinklers were on constant rotation. On winter mornings, white frost sheeted the buffalo grass. The village was largely populated with young single-income families, or older empty nesters whose families had lived in the area for generations. On the village outskirts lived an assortment of city dropouts in caravans or small fibro houses backing directly onto bushland. Then there were the market gardeners, who largely kept to themselves, including a small number of Maltese, Italian and Chinese immigrants who'd brought one or two acres of cheap land and worked it for their living.

In Kellyville village everybody knew everybody. Bordeaux and Cleopatra Clarke, the young black couple who'd purchased the little blonde-brick house next to old Betty and Jack's place on Hectare Street, were the most bizarre of blow-ins. They weren't like the market gardener migrants; they'd bought *inside the village*, right in the thick of things. Bordy could be seen mowing the lawn of a Saturday morning, thick glasses fogged up with perspiration, black muscles shining from underneath his dark blue Bonds singlet, striped terry-towelling sweatband circling his afro. His tight denim shorts raised the eyebrows of many a passer-by. Then there was Cleopatra, ever-stylish in her head wraps, earrings and boots. 'An actress,' people whispered to each other. 'That's what old Betty heard her say.' And their English, that was perhaps the biggest oddity of all: so perfectly spoken. That was not how the locals expected black folk to talk. Heads were scratched. Fences were stared over. Gossip was spread.

There was history in it, though, this Africa-descended migration, if the new arrivals or their neighbours had only known. Among the convicts brought on the First Fleet to help build the new colony were several men of African descent, some likely hailing from the West Indies. On their release, these settlers of colour bought land, and brought up families, in Pennant Hills, not far from Kellyville. Over time, because of its inhabitants of colour, the area became known as Dixieland – named thus by white settlers after the region in America's Deep South which incorporated Mississippi, Alabama, Louisiana and the eight other states of the slave belt which made up the Confederate States of America from 1861 to 1865. At the time of Bordy and Cleo's arrival in Kellyville, though, the locals were likely unaware of this history. For many of them, Bordeaux and Cleopatra Clarke were the first black people they'd ever seen up close.

In these improbable surroundings, Bordy and Cleo's family grew. First came a daughter, Cecelia, in 1978. Eighteen months later came their middle child – me. And in 1982 a boy was born, Bronson. Their family was now complete.

By the early 1980s, race riots had again erupted across the UK, as a result of British police officers abusing stop and search laws to racially profile and unfairly target ethnic minorities – namely, young black men. Race relations, under the United Kingdom's new conservative prime minister, continued to be fraught. But none of this mess touched the little brick house on Hectare Street. The home Bordeaux and Cleopatra had made was packed with love, laughter, playdough and pride.

So went my early childhood. This is how it sang.

Hectare Street sat at the very edge of Kellyville village. Down the end of our road, some eight hundred metres or so from our front door, was a small creek. The rickety bridge that crossed it served as the border between the village and the small acreage properties beyond.

In summer, us children would troop denim-shorted and hypercolour t-shirted with Mum or Dad down to the creek, clutching glass jars or empty ice-cream containers. We'd scoop up the clear, shallow water until we had a sufficient number of wriggling black tadpoles. The tadpoles were then kept on the back veranda of our house. Sometimes we'd rear them long enough for their heads to fatten and their two back legs to develop. Inevitably, though, there would be some kind of mishap. The bucket would be accidentally kicked over, or an unexpected downpour would cause the containers to overflow, and that would be the end of our endeavour to hand-rear frogs.

On weekends, we would drive down the back of Kellyville and buy fruit and vegetables from the market gardeners. Out in the small fields, workers would be stooped low to the ground, triangular straw hats or water-soaked head wraps protecting them from the unforgiving sun. Out front of each small allotment was a makeshift stand – often just a few plastic milk crates stacked together – loaded up with freshly picked tomatoes or strawberries. Each had a cardboard sign with the price and a tin honesty box.

To add to the eccentric mix of the outer margin of the city, peppered among the standard three-bedroom blonde-bricks were Federation-style houses, all complete with chimneys but missing television aerials. These were the houses of the Exclusive Brethren, a fringe religious group whose Australian headquarters happened to be in the village. Their windowless church hall was perched righteously on the hill next to the local Catholic primary school on Hectare Street, while our unwaveringly atheist family lived at the bottom of the hill. Fitting, if amusing, geography.

Though our lives were worlds apart, I empathised with the Brethren children from an early age. They, too, had been thrust unexpectedly into this close-knit village, and were highly visible due to their different behaviour and old-fashioned attire. On Friday nights, the Brethren were duty-bound to proselytise, the head preacher (inevitably a tubby-around-the-middle ageing male) ranting about hellfire and damnation to bemused families queuing for fish and chips outside Nick's Milk Bar on the Windsor Road shopping strip. Young Brethren women, skirts down to their ankles, cream blouses buttoned tightly at their wrists and necks, hair in rag curlers underneath their compulsory scarfs in preparation for the gathering later that night, provided a chorus of *amens* and *praise the Lords*.

'The Lord can see everything, sinners.' The preacher would point an accusing finger at a King Gee–clad man ferrying newspaper-wrapped hamburgers home to his young family.

'Amen, the Lord sees all!' the Brethren women would murmur in agreement.

'The Lord hears everything, sinners!'

'Amen, brother.'

'Everything!'

'Oh yes, the Lord, he surely hears!'

My toddler brother, Bronson, my already-at-school older sister, Cecelia, and I would listen to the dire warnings drifting in through the open window of our family's white Ford Falcon as we waited for Mum to hurry back from the milk bar with our fish and chips.

'Everything! The Lord hears. Everything!'

What the Lord was supposed to have heard and disapproved of in the ultra-conservative bible belt of Kellyville was anyone's guess.

3.

IN 1983, AT the age of four, I started at the local preschool. Kids attended for several half-days a week. Clag glue, poster paint, nap-time mats and morning-tea fruit were the order of the day. The play yard was lush and green, and contained play equipment fashioned out of wooden logs and old car tyres. I'd suffered tantrum-prompting envy at my older sister Cecelia's entry into 'big school' the previous year, and had been eagerly looking forward to a kingdom of my own. I was also happy to escape temporarily the curious crawling expeditions of my one-year-old brother.

But in every Eden lurks a serpent, and in this paradise, the joy-killer came in the form of a little girl named Carlita Allen. Tiny, freckle-faced, ash-blonde, rough-around-the-edges Carlita looked like she'd just stepped out of a glossy illustrated copy of *Seven Little Australians*. She was a Judy type: hardy, resolute, bold. The youngest in a family of three girls, she lived on one of Kellyville's bush properties. Carlita was talkative and ballsy. By all accounts, we should have fast become friends. But from the moment she laid eyes on me, Carlita Allen decided she didn't like me, and Carlita Allen made it *known*.

As the excited gaggle of four-year-olds lined up near the mulberry tree for our first day at preschool, Carlita Allen looked me up and down. Hand still clutching her mother's, she examined me from head to toe. I stared back hopefully, waiting for a verdict to register on her face. Her right eyebrow slowly levitated into her forehead. She raised her right hand to her hip. Finally, a haughty sneer inched its way across the upper left corner of her mouth.

Carlita Allen leaned towards me. 'You,' she whispered loudly, 'are *brown*.'

It wasn't as if I hadn't realised this very obvious difference between our family and almost all of the other people we knew. My skin colour was simply a concrete matter of fact, much like the sky was blue. Carlita was right: I *was* brown. But until that very moment, holding my mother's hand under the mulberry tree's enormous fan-like leaves, it never occurred to me that being *brown*, rather than the pale pinkish of most of my friends and neighbours, was in any way relevant to anything.

There lurked, in this small girl's declaration, an implied deficiency. I was in no doubt that there was something *wrong* with being *brown*, that being *brown* was not a very desirable thing at all. I craned my neck to look up at my mother, who in turn looked over at Carlita's mother. Mrs Allen shrugged and smiled. She picked a cotton thread from her peach-coloured blouse. She held the thread out between thumb and forefinger.

'Children are so honest, aren't they?' The thin cotton wisp floated slowly down to the ground.

Tension crept into my mother's body. She turned her head and started chatting to the mother on the other side of her. I turned the comment over in my head. On the one hand, Carlita had simply stated a fact. On the other, the way in which she'd stated it had raised a whole lot of questions I really didn't understand or know how to go about constructing answers to.

Despite the palpable visual differences of our family, my mother did everything she could to integrate us into our surroundings. Our entire neighbourhood seemed to orbit around my Mum: the school canteen worker, the infants school gross motor volunteer, local fete organiser and office holder for the Kellyville Reciprocal Babysitting Club. The front room in our house seemed a hub for neighbourhood gossip and gatherings.

On rare occasions, though, I would see another side of my mother. We'd be somewhere local – in the Castle Hill shopping mall searching for winter pyjamas, or piling into the car one Saturday after Little Athletics, and suddenly Mum would freeze and her eyes would widen. Then all three of us kids would suddenly be unbuckled at the speed of light and bustled across the road, or shovelled into a shopping trolley and wheeled at great haste over to the other side of Kmart. We came to recognise the cause of these urgent movements: my mother had spied, lurking conspicuously on the periphery of our whitewashed lives, another black woman.

My mother's excitement at the prospect of a kindred spirit wasn't surprising, given the vibrant black community from which she and my father had come. Here, in these rare encounters, was a glimpse of that other world she'd left behind. My brother, sister and I would hang around, bored, through exclamations and interrogations, as details were swapped, future visits arranged. My mother was always uncharacteristically quiet after chance meetings of this kind; she'd be absent-minded and aloof, as if her thoughts had wandered elsewhere. Cleo had agreed to move to the other side of the world so that my father could take up a lectureship at an Australian university. Mostly, she seemed at peace with the decision, but if ever she questioned her contentment with her new life, it would be in the days after her encounter with another black woman.

A visit would usually follow. Inevitably there'd be other black children present. Directed by the adults to *go play outside*, we'd stand gaping at each other: *them* and *us* – total strangers somehow expected to instantaneously bond as kin. As with any family gatherings of this kind, there were sometimes connections: firm friendships forged which continued into adulthood. Then there were those other encounters – in which, despite our mirrored knotty afros, confrontational pouts and way-too-smart-for-Aussie-children special-occasion attire, the children we visited with were as unlike us as the local louts who threw stones at us down at the BMX track around the corner from our house. It made no sense to me to equate *brown* with kinship, but nor did I expect being brown to disqualify me from friendship with those who weren't – those like Carlita Allen.

The two preschool teachers walked along the row of variously excited and woeful new arrivals, introducing themselves cheerily, gently prying chubby fingers from parents' legs and waving away tearful mothers. As they did, I tallied up the other *brown* people I saw on a daily basis. There were a few family friends of varying shades, perhaps ten or so. I saw people on the telly sometimes, on the news, or in the running races my father liked to watch. The telly was black and white though, so I could never *really* be sure. I saw brown folks in the newspapers some mornings, little kids even. But they were mostly so swollen-bellied and sad-looking that I didn't feel I was anything like them at all. The fact remained though: I *was* brown. And most of my world wasn't.

Carlita Allen's declaration wasn't just a passing observation. It was the source of all she disliked about me. Our first meal at preschool consisted of fruit and raisin toast, arranged on two large platters and placed in the centre of a long table made up of smaller, pushed-together kiddie tables. Our initial nervousness mostly forgotten, little hands flew quickly from platter to mouth and back again, until there was only one lonely piece of fruit left on the platter directly in front of me. Never one to turn down the opportunity for a feed, I closed my fingers around the ripe piece of pear and hustled it into my mouth. Carlita, seated diagonally across the table from me, rose to her feet so quickly that the chair behind her toppled over.

'You,' she said, pointing a finger accusingly, 'are greedy *and* brown.'

Later in the day, as we sat cross-legged in a circle, our beaming teachers invited us to recount to the group nice things we'd discovered about each other during our first day of preschool.

'Macthine hath lovely curly hair,' offered a girl named Bella. 'And thee ith very friendly.'

'She does, doesn't she? I've always wanted curly hair too,' one of the teachers responded.

'Yes, and being friendly is great!' the other enthused.

'She only has curly hair because she's *brown*.' Carlita sulkily twirled a strand of her own blonde mop around her finger.

The teachers fell silent for a moment, their eyes locking across the circle.

Little rosy-cheeked, ringlet-haired, lisping Bella, who would become one of my closest preschool allies, became a regular target for Carlita Allen.

'You can't even *talk* properly,' Carlita Allen informed her in the second week of preschool. By this stage, I had become partially immune to Carlita's brown-frowns, employing the *sticks and stones* mantra my mother had the foresight to revisit with me at home. Bella, though, was a timid girl. In the face of Carlita Allen's disdain, she came to dread preschool.

I would watch in the mornings as my friend's mother prised the screaming girl from her legs and hurried off, teary-eyed, struggling to shut out her daughter's broken-hearted howl. After several weeks of this, I decided to put my sandal-clad foot down, heading for the place I knew was the primary source of all knowledge and truth-telling.

'Carlita Allen at preschool is nasty to everyone,' I complained, standing barefoot in my frilly red-and-white shortie pyjamas on the flower-shaped tiles of our lime-green kitchen.

My mother opened a tin of apricot nectar; started browning chicken in a saucepan.

'She's always saying I'm brown and telling Bella she can't talk properly. She's nasty. None of us want to play with her anymore.'

'I'm not surprised,' Mum said offhandedly, turning the heat down under the sweet-smelling sauce, as she gently nudged my brother from around her leg. 'That sounds perfectly reasonable. It sounds like Carlita Allen is a big *bully*, and nobody wants to spend time with a bully.'

I wandered into the lounge room to mull the conversation over while I watched *Inspector Gadget*. As usual, my mother was absolutely right.

The next day, when I arrived at preschool, Bella was already in the classroom tucking into a piece of raisin bread. She was sitting underneath the hanging row of pegged-up finger-paintings we'd done of ourselves the day before. My smiling mud-brown face stared out at me from among the other light-pink-painted faces.

'Carlita ithn't here yet,' Bella stated firmly. Her fingers were shiny with melted butter. 'I hope thee doethn't come today.'

'That's perfectly reasonable,' I reassured my friend. 'Carlita Allen is a big bully. And *nobody* –' I emphasised the word the way I'd heard my mother's intonation change the evening before '– wants to play with a bully.'

One of the preschool teachers came over to ask whether I wanted some fruit bread too. I declined, and took myself off to stand just inside the front gate. Several of the other children arrived, their parents looking at me curiously as I stood determinedly at my post. I'd put on my bright red Minnie Mouse t-shirt that morning, which always made me feel extra gutsy.

Eventually, Mrs Allen's white car pulled into the car park. She opened the driver-side door and swung her stockinged legs and strappy gold shoes out onto the gravel. I watched nervously as she opened the back door for her daughter, grabbing Carlita's pink backpack from the back seat and handing it to her as she climbed out of the car.

'Hello,' she greeted me as she unlatched the gate. 'Are you waiting for somebody?'

'Yes,' I replied hesitantly. 'I'm waiting for Carlita.'

'Oh.' The woman looked down at her daughter, bemused. 'That's . . . nice.'

'Why is she waiting for me?' Carlita rolled her eyes in my direction. 'I don't *like* her. She's *brown*.'

'Carlita . . .' her mother reprimanded her vaguely, primping her fringe.

'That's okay,' I replied. 'I *am* brown. And I don't care if you don't like me, because I don't like you either. Neither does Bella. Neither do most of the other kids. And we don't want to play with you anymore. You're nasty. Don't come near us today. Play by yourself.'

'I beg your pardon?' Mrs Allen glared at me.

I was a little scared now, but I wasn't going to walk away before I'd said my piece.

'That's not very nice.' Mrs Allen raised her voice indignantly. 'How dare you say something like that to Carlita? Maxine, you are a very, very nasty little . . . little . . . black . . . girl.'

It wasn't just a how-dare-you, it was a how-dare-*you*? Her lips curled when she said that *you*, the same way Carlita's did when she said *brown*. I knew I wasn't nasty, and I didn't care if stuffy old Carlita Allen's mother, who wore ridiculous high-heeled shoes and had an even more ridiculous fanned-out fringe, thought I was.

'I'm not nasty,' I clarified. 'We just don't like Carlita. And that's perfectly reasonable. Because Carlita is a big *bully*, and *no-one* likes to play with bullies.'

'You horrible, *horrible* little girl,' Mrs Allen hissed down at me. 'You little . . . you little black . . . you apologise to Carlita *right* this minute.'

I was floored. I didn't feel I had anything to apologise for. But when a grown-up yelled at me like that, which wasn't very often, I was programmed to recant. Carlita stood there, just inside the fence, her Strawberry Shortcake bag on her back, smirking at me from behind her mother. I took a deep breath, looked down at my feet. 'Sorry.'

'You *look* at Carlita when you're speaking to her. And speak up so she can hear you properly!' Carlita's mother was yelling now, her face red with anger. There was a curtness in her voice which stung the same way the back of my thighs felt when Dad curtailed my cheekiness with a sudden slap.

'Sorry, Carlita.' I looked up, my right hand involuntarily flexing into a fist by my side.

'That's okay,' Carlita allowed smugly.

'Now you hold hands and walk her into class, and you make sure you play with her today and don't say anything else nasty.' Mrs Allen shook her head from side to side, still glaring at me.

My hand grew sweaty in Carlita's as we walked side by side up the path towards the preschool buildings. I felt like I would burst with the unfairness of it – as if the air around me was pushing hard into my skin, bearing down. When we reached the classroom door, I dropped Carlita's hand and looked back at her mother. Mrs Allen was still standing halfway up the front path, staring in our direction.

Sometimes, when we were at the grocery store, or somewhere else we needed to shop, me and Mum and Bronson and Cecelia would be waiting in a line for what seemed like hours. Other customers would come and go. Even those behind us would be served. It was as if the shopkeeper couldn't see us. It didn't happen often, but when it did, my mother would stand there quietly, her breath heaving in and out as if she was struggling to keep calm.

'That's not fair, Mum,' one of us would occasionally pipe up. Or perhaps, 'That lady pushed in front of us!' It was as if my mother didn't notice the rudeness, though. Even when she was finally served, she would just smile politely and we'd be on our way. I wondered, suddenly, if this was what she felt like all those times, this smouldering stifled rage. Anger burned in my throat.

4.

THE LOCAL PRIMARY school had been established way back in 1849. I started there as a student some hundred and thirty-six years later, in 1985. The school block sloped gradually downwards from the front entrance on Windsor Road – the main arterial road which runs all the way from the closest city of Parramatta, through North Rocks and Baulkham Hills, right through Kellyville and out the other side to the rural properties of Windsor and Rouse Hill.

Also on Windsor Road, not two hundred metres from the school's front gate, was Kellyville's main shopping strip: a small cluster of shops, including a milk bar, newsagency, chemist, bakery, deli, hardware shop and several eateries. The morning bus to the local high school left from outside the Kellyville shops. When we walked to school, we would wind through the suburban streets till we reached the back gate, but on the odd occasion us kids scored a lift from Mum, she would drop us at the front gate. We would stare curiously at the high school students. They milled around in their light blue collared shirts and dark blue skirts and shorts, their bags hanging casually off their shoulders.

Their language was peppered with profanities. They laughed and shrieked, and sometimes even smooched or held hands. Some of them munched on hot newspaper-wrapped potato scallops from Nick's, even though it was eighty-thirty in the morning.

The upper primary section of my school, which housed grades three to six, was a double-storey brick and concrete L-shaped building. A square concrete-paved courtyard was nestled into the inside of the L. This was where the primary students would line up every morning to file into class, and where weekly assemblies were held in the warmer months.

'*This is our school*,' we would chorus, as we recited the Monday morning creed, a fidgeting mass of red-and-white-checked tunics, nose-picking, scab-scratching, grey shorts, bandaids-on-knees and freckled faces huddled together on the hot concrete. '*Let peace dwell here. Let the room be full of happiness. Let love abide here: love of God, love of one another, and love of life itself . . .*'

Around the edges of the courtyard were wooden seats, over-hung by majestic clusters of gum trees. This was where the students would sit to eat lunch before running off to play skipping or handball or heading down the back of the school block to play chasings or weave daisy chains.

The infants section of the school, which housed kindergarten and grades one and two, was a cluster of three separate buildings further down the school grounds, each containing two classrooms, surrounded by similar seat-and-gum-tree clusters. There was a grass play area and wooden playground equipment. Cement toilet blocks and bubbler huts accompanied both the upper and lower primary school playgrounds.

On most weekday mornings, Dad would rise early for work, and Mum would get Cecelia and me ready for school. Then my sister and I would walk to school past neat brick and fibro houses, their closely clipped lawns planted with bright red bottlebrushes and hot pink busy lizzies. Past classmates, also walking. Past safety house signs on letterboxes, and mighty come-climb-me oaks, gnarled arms heavy with acorns. Cecelia and I were like chalk and cheese, despite there being only an eighteen-month age gap. Once we entered the school gate, we'd go our separate ways. There was a silent solidarity in our approach, though: a mutual bracing against the day ahead.

It had taken just a few months at preschool, up against the constant jeers of Carlita Allen and any other kids she managed to co-opt in her anti-brown crusade, to wise up to the perils of exclusion. I knew before I started big school that, for me, the playground would be a battlefield: a world divided into allies and enemies. At five and a half, racism had already changed me.

After a while, you start to breathe it. Another kid's parents stare over at your family on the first day of school with *that* look on their faces. You make a mental note to stay away from that kid. When you have to choose working partners in numbers, you discreetly shuffle over to the opposite side of the room. You tell a teacher someone is calling you names. *Blackie. Monkey girl. Golliwog.* The teacher stares at you, exasperated, as if to say: *Do you really expect me to do something about it?* The next time you have a grievance, you look for a different teacher. This is how it changes us. This is how we're altered.

The way my mother tells it, I was always the easy middle child: no-nonsense, happy-go-lucky, low maintenance, cheery and friendly. Back then though, even in early primary school,

I was intrinsically aware that the more invisible I was, the easier my life would become.

Despite the name-calling, and being picked last for most activities, I loved kindergarten. I had arrived at school already reading. *Learning things* excited me. The brightly stained counting blocks, letter tracing sheets and sentence-maker boards in my first classroom were like some kind of heaven. Yet the quiet longing for acceptance that had been seeded the moment Carlita Allen had told me I was *brown* and she *didn't like it* had taken root.

In grade one, I was really looking forward to being Student of the Week. Each Monday, Mrs Kingsley would pull one of our names out of a glass jar on her desk and write it on the board, and the kid whose name was drawn would become Student of the Week. The Student of the Week got special privileges, like being able to pick their working partner, and being called on first to choose art materials or reading books. The Student of the Week would stand out the front of the class, and the teachers would ask them to *please tell the class a little bit about yourself.* Then the whole class got to ask questions, like what kind of pet they had at home and what their favourite colour was.

Finally, in the middle of second term, my name was pulled out of the jar.

'Maxine Clarke!' The teacher beamed across the room at me as I stood up from my yellow plastic chair and made my way to the front of the room. I turned to face the class. My best friend Jennifer, who sat next to me in class, was smiling encouragingly at me from our shared desk.

Mrs Kingsley adjusted her glasses. 'Do you want to start by telling us about yourself?' she asked.

'My favourite colour is yellow,' I declared. 'I have one sister and one brother. And my favourite food is chocolate. And I have two pet guinea pigs. And I live in Kellyville.' I took a deep breath. 'I started a dance class last week, but I don't like it very much. Jennifer is my best friend. I do piano lessons but I don't like them very much either. I really like the grape flavour of Hubba-Bubba bubble gum. It's my favourite.' I stopped for a few seconds to think. 'My best season that I like is spring because my birthday is in spring. My best fruit that I like is watermelon. My mum is an actress, and my dad is a mathematician. He does very hard things with very difficult numbers. One time a man at his work where he does numbers told me he has an *amazing mind*. He came up to me and said, *Your dad has an AMAZING mind!* like that. My little brother is sometimes very naughty. Whenever we go to visit my dad at his work where he does maths, he—'

'Okay, thanks, Maxine!' Mrs Kingsley cut me off.

I glared at her angrily. I wanted the other kids to know *everything* about me — all of the things they hadn't asked because I was just the brown kid. Today was my one opportunity to let everyone know I wasn't just that.

'I wasn't finished!' I pouted, crossing my arms.

'Well, I have a few questions already!' Mrs Kingsley said brightly.

I stared at her, waiting.

'Is your mum *really* an actress, darling?' she asked in a gentle voice.

'Yes. I went to a play that she did once in a big theatre. There were chickens onstage, in a cage.' I could still remember how strange it had been, to see my mum pretending to be somebody else, in front of all of those people; I could remember the plush red seats at the theatre in the city; the bags of red Jaffas my dad had let us buy.

'I think you have a *very vivid* imagination. And what does your father really do for a job?'

'He's a mathematician.' Maybe I'd got the word wrong. It was a very hard word. Perhaps I wasn't saying it right. 'He does maths, like when we do numbers in class. Only much harder. At a *university*.' Sometimes, in the school holidays, Cecelia and I had to go in to work with Dad. He'd sit us up the back of the enormous lecture theatre, with lollies and colouring books, and we'd have to be very quiet while he talked loudly and scrawled dots and numbers and strange-looking symbols across the blackboard with white chalk for the hundreds of adult students who had come to hear him speak.

Mrs Kingsley smiled and shook her head slightly from side to side, as if she didn't quite know what to do with me. 'I think we'll have to get your parents in here on Careers Day, to talk about what they actually do. Your mum stays home and minds your little brother, doesn't she? So, does anyone else want to ask Maxine a question?' Mrs Kingsley had now moved to the back of the classroom.

'I wasn't finished, Mrs Kingsley. I have more to tell about myself!'

Ignoring my protests, the teacher looked around the class. Lewis Stevens was staring out the window. Carlita Allen was whispering to the girl next to her. A boy in the front row was digging his finger deep into his nostril.

'I shall ask another question then!' Mrs Kingsley said. Mrs Kingsley was old. *Really* old. Older than my nannas even, I reckoned. She walked slowly, had a silver-blue shine to her roller-set hair, and always used words like *shall*, and *may* and *jolly* and *rather*, like in Enid Blyton books.

'Where are you from?' my teacher asked brightly.

'Pardon, Mrs Kingsley?'

'Where are you from?'

Unsure of the answer she wanted, I stared at her for a moment. 'From my mum's tummy,' I replied matter-of-factly.

A faint titter of amusement ran around the room. The class was suddenly extremely attentive.

'That's not what I meant, Maxine,' said my teacher curtly.

I stared at her, confused.

'The class is interested in where you're from, Maxine,' she said insistently.

I racked my brain, staring at the clear plastic boxes of counting blocks stacked up on the bookshelf behind Mrs Kingsley. I imagined myself tipping them all out, fashioning them into a Lego-like ladder and climbing away out of the classroom window.

'From my mum's . . . *vagina?*' I said tentatively.

The class erupted into giggles.

'You *rude* girl!' Mrs Kingsley looked furious. 'You *know* what I am asking. Why are you being so *insolent*? What country were you born in?'

'This one.' My head was hurting now.

'Oh,' said Mrs Kingsley 'Well . . . where are your parents from?'

'They came here from England.'

Mrs Kingsley was glaring at me again. A boy called Matthew, who was sitting at the back of the room, right next to where our teacher was standing, started laughing.

'They're not from England!' he said scathingly. 'My nanna's from England and your parents are *not like her*. They're not English, Mrs Kingsley!'

Maxine Beneba Clarke

I knew my parents had come to Australia from England. I had even been back there when I was smaller, to visit my grandparents and cousins. I remembered a bit of it. There were photos of me and Cecelia and Bronson on a sled in the snow with our gumboots and parkas on.

'I want you to go home and ask your parents where they're from,' said my teacher. 'And you can come back and tell us properly tomorrow. Does anyone have any other questions?'

Rebecca, a sweet pale-faced girl with red hair, raised her arm.

'Yes, Rebecca?' My teacher seemed relieved that the conversation was moving along.

'What do . . . people like you . . . *feel* like?'

'What do you mean, Rebecca?' Mrs Kingsley asked, exasperated. 'You'll have to explain the question to her a little better than that, darling.'

'I mean, do you have *normal* feelings . . . like normal people do?'

Silence fell over the classroom as all of the other six-year-olds waited eagerly for my answer. Outside the classroom window, a pack of galahs was tearing apart one of the gum trees, shrieking and squawking as they tore the nuts from the branches and dropped them onto the wooden seats below. I looked over at them for a moment, then back into the classroom. The three ceiling fans hummed as they whirred lopsidedly around.

'I don't know,' I said quietly. 'I don't know if I have normal feelings like normal people do.'

When my Student of the Week question time had finished, Mrs Kingsley asked me to choose a piece of A4 cardboard to use for my Student of the Week album. I chose a sunflower-yellow piece of card, and walked slowly back to my seat. The cardboard would be passed around the class that day, with each student

38

writing down something nice about me in brightly coloured pencil. At the end of the day, the poster would be pinned to the noticeboard, and at the end of the week, I'd get to take it home.

I watched, throughout the day, as the brightly coloured rectangle moved from desk to desk. Eventually, it landed on the desk next to mine. My best friend Jennifer slowly read down the page, looked over at me, picked up her pink pencil and began to write. She worked away for about ten minutes, stopping every now and then to think.

Jennifer was a shy girl with thin brown-blonde hair and a delicate sparrow-like face. Her family, the McGuires, had been one of the few that had welcomed my parents on their arrival in Kellyville, and us kids were frequently at their house playing with Jen and her brother and sister. Jen had been at preschool with me, and we started school at the same time. We never spoke about the differences between us, or about the indignities I suffered on account of them, but in my memories of early primary school Jen is always there, standing next to me, unmoving.

'Once you've finished, hand the album over to Maxine, please, dear,' Mrs Kingsley instructed. 'Then she can read it out and we can pin it up.'

Reluctantly, Jennifer handed me the piece of card. I ran my eyes down the misspelled comments.

Maxine is brown.

Maxine has brown skin.

Maxine has funny curly hair.

Maxine thinks her family is from England.

Maxine has dark brown skin.

Maxine is nice and Maxine is black.

Maxine is friendly.

Maxine is not Australian.

Maxine is brown and she does dancing.

Maxine has a black family and a little brother.

Maxine doesn't know about her feelings.

Maxine is brown.

She is brown.

She has brown skin.

At the bottom of the list was a whole paragraph written neatly in bright pink pencil.

'Stand up and read out your album, Maxine!' Mrs Kingsley said. 'I'm sure the class had some lovely things to write about you.'

I stood up, pushing my chair back away from the desk, and read out the one pink paragraph at the bottom, written by my friend Jennifer. '*Maxine is friendly and smart. She is a good reader. She plays the piano. She has a brother and a sister. She is very good at spelling. She is a happy girl, and I like to play with her. She is my friend.*'

'Well, isn't that nice?' said Mrs Kingsley. 'Would you like to pin the album up to remind us what a special student we have in our class this week?'

I paused for a moment. 'Can I please go to the toilet, Mrs Kingsley?'

'Okay . . . but you must be quick, dear. Pin the album up on the wall on your way out, please.'

I picked up the piece of cardboard, clutching it with both hands, and moved towards the door. Inside the empty girl's toilet block, I re-read my Student of the Week album then tore a jagged line between Jennifer's words and the other comments. I read Jennifer's words out loud to myself once, then twice, then four more times. I had never had anything written about me before, except for my kindergarten school reports and things the doctor wrote down in her folder when I was sick. The things Jennifer wrote were solid things now. She had grabbed them from the air when I spoke to the class, and listened to them. She had made them *real.* I didn't even care about the rest of the comments. I folded up the jagged bit of cardboard containing Jennifer's words, and zipped the small rectangle into my tunic pocket. I tore the rest of the page up into tiny pieces, opened the door to one of the toilet cubicles, and watched as the yellow flakes slowly turned to sog inside the toilet bowl.

I wanted people to write down more true things about me – wanted to start writing down stories about myself, *making* myself real: *making* other people see me. There was a rhyme my mother had told me at home which always confused me: *sticks and stones can break my bones, but words can never hurt me.* Names did hurt though. The *words* did hurt. They hurt deep inside my chest. They hurt inside my head. They hurt inside my heart.

I loved words, and I loved stories, but mostly the books in the school library were about princesses and princes and Spot the Dog. I loved them anyway, because they contained combinations of words that took me into other worlds, allowed me to escape for that brief moment of relief. But most of them weren't about people like me.

For our school's Book Week dress-up parade, my mother had encouraged us to go as characters that were the most like us. But Cecelia and I didn't want to go dressed as one of the characters from the few children's books we owned that had black kids in them. Nobody knew who Kojo from *Oh Kojo! How Could You?* was, in his brightly coloured African tunic top. Nobody knew who Liza Lou was, in her short, tattered sundress, *ferrying Sunday-go-to-meeting-finery* across the haunted *yeller belly swamp.*

Maxine Beneba Clarke

I had gone dressed as Pocahontas the first year, while Cecelia was Hiawatha: characters of colour the other kids might at least know.

Words had never before been about *me*, had never before made me feel as *good* as Jennifer's words on my Student of the Week album had made me feel. They had never before made me see that I *existed*; had never been so overtly and unashamedly *on my side*. Jennifer's words seemed powerful now that they were written down. Magical. Like they were forever.

5.

AT THE AGE of seven, my older sister Cecelia had already seen a dead body. Or she claimed she had, at least. This was the primary, though not the only, reason our mother wasn't so keen on her being best friends with Leonie Dalton. Leonie was a chubby girl with a sharp bob of straight jet-black hair and slightly tanned complexion which surely must have both harked back to a partial heritage no-one in Kellyville was game to query. Leonie was impossibly outgoing and very quirky for suburban Kellyville – due in no small part to overexposure to her father's vocation: she was the youngest child of a funeral director. During an afternoon playing at Leonie's house, or so she relayed it later that evening, my sister had tiptoed into the funeral parlour with her friend to lift the heavy wooden lid of a coffin and stare at the corpse of a waxen elderly lady awaiting burial.

'It's no big deal,' Cecelia said to us that evening with a shrug, as she recounted the incident over dinner. 'I mean, she just looked like she was sleeping. Only kind of greyer and saggier.' That West Indian way, of spinning a tale, or else what's a story for?

'Cecelia!' my mother had exclaimed, shaking her head in disbelief.

Months later, on Cecelia's eighth birthday, I sat opposite Leonie, in a circle of five or so of Cecelia's classmates, as she beamed at my sister and handed her a large parcel wrapped in pink foil paper. In our household, birthdays were a big deal, in that old-fashioned house-full-of-local-kids, egg-and-spoon-racing, parcel-passing, sack-racing way. The highlight was always the cake, which the birthday boy or girl got to choose from Mum's special *Women's Weekly* cake book. Each double-page spread contained a full-colour photograph of the finished cake and a collection of measurements, instructions and diagrams. There were fairy cakes, lorry trucks carrying liquorice logs, ballerinas mid-pirouette, caterpillars, rabbits, fairy princesses and aeroplanes. The book was kept at the back of the cupboard in our hallway, secreted away as if it contained powerful magic spells. For my sister's eighth birthday, a brown chocolate-cake ballerina with a pink-frosted tutu dotted with raspberry-lolly embellishments was the order of the day.

Mum was busy in the kitchen putting the finishing touches to the cake. The party guests sat in a small cross-legged circle around my sister on the khaki-and-white-flecked carpet of the bedroom Cecelia and I shared. We squirmed in anticipation as Cecelia struggled with the parcel Leonie had just handed her, which was entombed in lashings of sticky tape. My sister finally wrestled the present free from its wrapping, and let out an ear-piercing squeal of delight.

'A Cabbage Patch Kid! Oh my god! I got a Cabbage Patch Kid!'

Cabbage Patch Kids were the Toy You Had to Have. We'd never had a Toy You Had to Have before, though a Barbie and the Rockers Barbie would soon follow. Cecelia and I had been

44

harassing our mother about getting Cabbage Patch Kids for almost a year, but our desperation had fallen on decidedly unhearing ears.

'They're too expensive, too useless, and ugly,' was my mother's standard response when we mentioned the doll.

Cabbage Patch Kids *were* ugly, to the aesthetically judgemental eye. Their hard plastic faces swelled into impossibly round cheeks, which puckered into gummy smiles. Their painted-on eyes were wild and wide, like they were tripping out of their minds. Their soft polyester bodies were out of proportion to their enormous heads, and their feet were concealed in square plastic shoes that looked orthopaedic.

But all this was forgivable, because the Cabbage Patch Kids had an intriguing backstory. Legend had it Cabbage Patch Kids weren't made in a factory like other toys, but grew from the very earth we walked on. Xavier Roberts, the grandfather of all Cabbage Patch Kids, had picked each and every doll from the actual cabbage patch, which was located in some secret, unreachable corner of the world. Grandfather Roberts knew exactly which 'Mum' or 'Dad' the universe had grown each doll for, and yours would always find its way to you, because you were destined to be together. The toys came complete with an adoption certificate, bearing the doll's first and middle names. Once sent away for processing, the certificate was returned with the doll now bearing the surname of the child owner. In this way, the market for cheap knock-offs was also protected. Those with fake imposter dolls earned justifiable playground scorn.

Cecelia stopped gazing at the pug-faced doll and turned it around so the rest of the party guests could admire it. Our enthusiastic squeals could no doubt be heard halfway down Hectare Street. The Cabbage Patch Kid had long blonde hair, fashioned from thick yellow wool. It was wearing light blue terry-towelling tracksuit pants, which the party guests hastily pulled down to reveal the Xavier Roberts signature on the right cheek of the doll's bottom – another slightly creepy indicator of authenticity.

Surveying the scene, my face grew hot with jealousy. Leonie Dalton had now not only allowed my sister to see a dead body – a morbid adventure worthy of endless playground retellings – she'd also given her what I most coveted in the world.

Another of my sister's friends suddenly lunged over to grab at the doll. 'Oh my god! It has a tooth! This Cabbage Patch is real *and* it has a *tooth*!' She turned the doll back around to face the group, and pointed hysterically to the tiny TicTac-like piece of white plastic glued to the doll's puckered lips.

The circle collapsed in on itself. Girls scrambled to their feet, all other presents forgotten. I stayed where I was, sitting on the carpet, fighting back tears.

'Everything okay in here, girls?' My mother stood in the doorway, icing spatula in hand.

'Leonie gave Cecelia a Cabbage Patch Kid,' I said mournfully.

'Oh. That's nice.' My mother's attempt to sound enthusiastic was seriously lacklustre.

'A *real* one,' I continued pointedly. 'An expensive one with a signature on its bottom and a birth certificate signed by Xavier Roberts.'

'Wow!' Mum's voice was still flat.

'*And* it has a tooth,' I added.

'A tooth?' My mother came into the room, kneeled down beside me and patted my shoulder.

'The ones with teeth —' I paused to control the tremor in my voice '— are *very* rare and special.'

'Oh.'

'And —' I knew this would annoy my mother '— it has *blonde* hair. *Long, blonde* hair. Cecelia has a *blonde* doll.'

'Well . . . that's just lovely,' my mother said cautiously, smiling at the party guests who had now turned to face us, waiting for her to exhibit a suitably ecstatic reception to the gift. 'I'm sure Leonie put a lot of thought into choosing a present she knew Cecelia would love. Just like all you other girls did. Now, who's ready for cake?'

I couldn't believe it. After all of our mother's refusals to cave in to our whining about Cabbage Patch Kids, after all those lectures about how *ridiculously expensive* Cabbage Dolls were, *how hideous*, she wasn't even going to make Cecelia give the present back. Outraged, I followed my mother back down the hallway and into the kitchen.

'Mum . . .'

'Maxine, please, don't start,' she warned, pointing the spatula at me for a moment as she half turned from the ballerina cake she had been icing.

'But—'

'Not now!'

'But she got—'

'Look,' she said with a defeated sigh, 'I'll buy you a Cabbage Patch Kid, okay? You'll have to have it for your birthday and Christmas combined, though. And no other presents. They're just too expensive.'

'Thanks, Mum! That's okay — I don't want anything else.'

Maxine Beneba Clarke

For the next six months, my head was full of the promise of a Cabbage Patch Kid. I tried to imagine what she or he would be wearing, what the name on the birth certificate would be, whether it would have a tooth, curly hair, a dimple, or any other such rare and special feature that would render my doll unlike the dolls the other girls in Kellyville had. Although I speculated, I really couldn't have cared less what my doll looked like. I knew that was part of what was going to make me such a great mother. I would love him or her with all my heart, dimple or no dimple, gummy smile or toothy. As long as it had that birth certificate and signature of authenticity. As long as it was a *real* Cabbage Patch Kid.

'Make sure it has the signature on it, please,' I cautioned Mum regularly. 'Otherwise it's not a *real* Cabbage Patch.'

'Okay, Maxine, I get it,' she'd say, exasperated.

Sometimes I'd lie awake at night thinking about that first day when I'd turn up at school with the doll. There'd be a body jam at the back gate as all the kids ran to see what my doll looked like. All the girls who already had a Cabbage Patch Kid would want to come over to my house and play, so that their dolls could make friends with mine.

The night before my birthday I lay awake for hours, listening to the deafening vibrations of the cicadas as they shed their golden skins in the large bottlebrush tree outside our bedroom window. Neighbourhood dogs barked. John Farnham's 'You're the Voice' crooned from somebody's open window. As the street noise died down, the various creaks and whisperings of the house took over.

Finally, when I couldn't bear it any longer, I quietly swung my feet out from under my sheets and down onto the carpet. Across the room Cecelia shifted in her sleep, grinding her teeth

48

and muttering inaudibly. The hallway light was left on, as it always was, for night-time toilet trips. I crept around the corner into the kitchen. The clock revealed it was already one in the morning – *technically* my birthday.

I squinted through the darkness into the kitchen and could just make out the shape of the parcel sitting on the table. Wrapped in bright orange paper with a pale blue bow, it was the only present on the table, and the exact size and shape of the box a Cabbage Patch Kid came in. I sighed happily and turned to make my way back to bed, then faltered. I wouldn't be able to sleep for wondering what the doll looked like, and it would be almost five hours before anyone else would be awake to open it with me.

I walked slowly over to the table and slid a forefinger carefully underneath the wrapping paper. One end of the parcel came loose. I raised the still-wrapped end of the parcel and slid the box towards the open end. Plastic white shoes gleamed out at me. Then adorable purple-striped white slacks. Then a ruffled pink-and-purple jacket. Out of the cuffs of the jacket poked my new baby's chubby Cabbage Patch hands. Only there was something wrong with her hands. They didn't *look* like any Cabbage Patch hands I'd ever seen. They were the same shape and size, but there was something not normal about them. They were *brown* hands.

I slid the doll completely out of the wrapping and stared at her, overcome with disappointment. It was a Cabbage Patch Kid alright, the adoption certificate clearly displayed at the back of the box said so: *Wenona Jane Clarke, adopted by Maxine Beneba Clarke.* It still had the same wide Cabbage Patch Kid eyes, the same signature on the bum in loopy cursive writing, and long, dark brown hair fashioned from wool. But I didn't want a brown Cabbage Patch Kid. I hadn't *asked* for a brown Cabbage Patch Kid.

Nobody I had ever met had a *brown* Cabbage Patch Kid. Where did Mum even find this thing? Every girl in grade one would be waiting to see the Cabbage Patch I'd been talking about for months, and *this* was what I'd have to show them.

Faint footsteps started up at the far end of the house. I could sense my mother, standing in the kitchen doorway behind me.

'I thought it would be you,' she whispered. 'Happy Birthday!'

Without turning, I could tell she was smiling, waiting for my excitement. I swallowed past the lump in my throat, straightened up, turned to face her.

'Thanks, Mum.' I kissed her cheek, gave her a hug.

'That's okay. I hope you like her! Back to bed now.' She gently pushed me in the direction of my room. 'Why don't you take your doll to bed with you?' she suggested, removing it from the box and following me up the hallway. 'After all, it's already your birthday.'

'Yeah, okay. Good idea.' I forced another smile as she lowered the freak creature into my arms.

I lay underneath the thin cotton sheet, staring at the brown face of the doll. She was ugly. I hated her.

'Aren't you going to take your new doll with you?' Mum asked, as Cecelia and I rushed out the door to school the next morning. She hurried back into the house, came out with the Cabbage Patch Kid. 'I'm sure all the other girls would love to play with it to!'

I reached for Wenona, took my lunchbox, pencil case and school hat out of my bag, shoved her right to the bottom, and put my other school things on top of her. I zipped up my schoolbag and wrestled it onto my back. When I looked up, Mum was still standing on the front steps of our house, staring at me with a strange look on her face.

'Where's your Cabbage Patch Kid?' asked one of my classmates as we unpacked our red schoolbags in the cloakroom.

'Here it is!' Carlita, whose designated bag hook was stationed next to mine, wrenched the doll from inside my bag and waved it above her head. 'Look! Maxine has a *brown* doll! Look at it! It's *so* ugly!'

The other kids unpacking their bags in the cloakroom turned to look. I squeezed my eyes shut, waiting for the exclamations of disgust.

Susana, another of the girls in my class, rescued the doll from Carlita. 'Of course it's brown,' she said, looking it over. 'It's the one that was grown especially for *her*. It's *her* kid.'

'I've never seen a brown one before,' another girl said. 'Pass it over here!'

'I've seen one. Rudy on *The Cosby Show* has two of them.'

'Yeah, Rudy has one like that.'

'Here, put it next to mine.' Another girl fished her Cabbage Patch Kid out of her backpack, brought it over next to mine. 'Let's see how different they look.'

'It's *ugly*,' Carlita repeated.

'Go away, Carlita,' Susana said firmly.

My Cabbage Patch Kid was suddenly shoved back into my hands. The gaggle of girls descended, pushing and shoving, to get a closer look.

———

By the mid-eighties Australia was slowly changing. We would glimpse, my family and I, other people of colour more often:

Chinese, Fijian, Vietnamese, Indian – at the local shops or driving down our street. Even if no words passed between us, ever-so-subtle signs of acknowledgement would be exchanged between the adults. That *we see you* nod. That *we know your life* smile. That *it's not easy* wave.

My parents began to gather around us a close group of friends from all different parts of the world. They were born in places I'd never heard of: India, Italy, Sri Lanka, Bolivia, Germany, Uganda. They were teachers, scientists, cooks, nurses and academics. As well as weekend get-togethers, so us kids could get to know each other, the grown-ups would meet for dinner parties at each other's houses. When the gatherings were held at our house, Cecelia, Bronson and I would hang around the kitchen sneaking soft white dinner rolls and after-dinner mints until shooed off to bed. I would lie under the covers, listening to the tumbling cacophony of accents as the adults laughed, argued and talked long into the evening.

As well as increased multiculturalism, another legacy of the Whitlam era, Aboriginal land rights, was coming to fruition. After years of campaigning, Uluru, the giant sandstone formation in the Northern Territory, sacred to the Indigenous people of the area, which had come to be known by white folks as the tourist attraction Ayers Rock, was finally returned to its traditional owners.

In our house on Hectare Street, we watched the handover on the evening news. I was sitting on a giant yellow cushion at Mum's feet, while she sat on the couch behind me, braiding my hair into cornrows for the school week. There were people on the television – *black people* – standing around in the desert, with some white men in suits. The black people looked like they were happy, celebrating. They waved a flag I hadn't seen before: divided in two horizontally, with a big round circle in the middle.

'Who are those . . . *people*?' I asked Mum, as she rubbed Blue Magic moisturiser into my afro and combed out the knots with a wooden fork comb.

'They're the Aboriginal people,' Mum explained, sliding the edge of the comb along my scalp to section my thick curls into six even parts running from my forehead down to my neck. 'They're the *original* Australians. They lived here before any white people came.' She gathered three strands of hair together, and began to twist them round each other into a braid.

I stared straight ahead, squinting at the slightly fuzzy images on our tiny black-and-white television screen. She must be mistaken, I thought. Where were these *original people*? I had never heard of them before. If this really was their country, why didn't they show themselves to me? If brown people owned the country, that would change *everything*. Besides, I was sure I would have learned about it at school, if it were true. I dismissed the conversation as some kind of misunderstanding.

Along with *The Cosby Show*, which showed a black family similar to mine in a lot of ways, came *Play School*'s Trisha Goddard. Trisha was a black woman full of stories and nursery rhymes and dances, who looked and sounded a little like my mum.

And out of nowhere, a young brown girl popped up on a computer game advertisement on television one evening. Wearing a funky white jacket and white cut-off jeans, she flipped her ringlets about as she high-kicked and sashayed with a group of super-cool kids in sunglasses. '*What do I want?*' she sang soulfully.

'*I want the sounds that curl my hair! What do we want? We want Atari!*' Behind her, a large clunky computer screen showed a Pac-Man-like computer game. I stopped what I was doing and ran to watch every time I heard her voice coming from the TV.

Then, one Saturday morning, a graceful doe-like young black woman named Whitney Houston appeared on *Video Hits*. She sang into the camera with dreamy almond eyes, wearing a clingy light purple dress and carefully layered bright pink and blue eye shadow. Her long, frizzy afro hair was dyed orange-blonde. Whitney Houston said she wanted to dance with somebody, with somebody who loved her. Whitney was black, and she was *beautiful*, and somehow, hers didn't seem like such an unlikely proposal.

6.

THERE ARE SOME sports people of African descent don't generally excel at. Swimming is the first that springs to mind. Some say it's physiological – to do with muscle density, bone mass and skeletal structure. Sometimes I wonder if it's in fact related to muscle memory – the intergenerational trauma passed on in our genes. It was always the sea that brought bloodshed to our lands; the ocean on which they arrived to destroy us; the tide on which they stole us away.

The watery tracks of my family's unbelonging scar this great, green globe like keloid geography. For centuries, our blood has crisscrossed the cobalt blue: backwards and forwards, north to south, circling in search of a safe landing space. From the west coast of Africa to the Jamaican harbour of Port Royal and the Guyanese capital of Georgetown. From the orange heat of the Caribbean to the bleak docks of England. Then, soaring high over white cumulus cloud towards a new life down south in Australia.

My father used to joke that black people were like oil, or Teflon: naturally resistant to water. But perhaps deep in these veins is this memory of leaving a hundred homes: involuntarily, reluctantly, desperately. *Anxiously.* Neither one of my parents could swim much more than a few metres of breaststroke. Perhaps it was their own fear of water that made them insist that their children take swimming lessons every summer school holidays at our local pool.

The local outdoor swimming pool was all thigh-scalding concrete bleachers and grungy changing rooms with there-since-forever hairs caught around the shower plugholes. The toilet floors were always wet with pool water from peeled-off swimmers and who knew what else. The only salvation was the pool kiosk, stocked with banana Paddle Pops, Ovalteenies in orange foil packets and fifty-cent paper bags of chewy red and green frog lollies.

Cecelia, Bronson and I hated swimming lessons, and though we didn't look forward to returning to school at the end of the summer holidays, the start of the first school term signalled the end of swimming lessons, and our return to extracurricular activities we could nominate ourselves.

My mother had a rule that each of us children could do one extracurricular sports activity per term. The activities we chose often differed greatly from term to term; in the early days, most were extremely flash-in-the-pan.

Perhaps most disastrous was the ill-fated term my sister and I begged to join Debbie's Dynamic Dance Academy. Debbie's Dance took place in the big upstairs hall of the Kellyville Sports and Recreation Centre on Memorial Avenue. All the popular girls at school went to Debbie's: the loud, brash girls with sun-kissed skin and wavy blonde hair. The straight-backed, confident girls whose wide, white smiles and stone-washed denim weekend wear made them look like the kids in the Kmart catalogues that came through our letterbox. The fifth and sixth grade beauties who already shaved their legs and kissed the cute boys down the back of the playground at lunchtime. Debbie's Dance was the domain of the girls who won the school talent quest every single year: shimmering brilliantly in front of the whole school with enthusiastic jazz-hand flourishes, glowing smiles, hot green leggings and high side ponytails.

At Debbie's you got to wear a shiny electric blue leotard with a rectangular black mesh panel across the middle which showed off your belly-button. This risqué costume was one of the primary motivations for us seeking enrolment. It took Cecelia and I about ten minutes to tire of sashaying diagonally across the room while glancing admiringly at our reflections in the studio mirrors, but Mum had decreed that once we were enrolled in an activity, we had to attend for the entire term. This was both to give each activity a fair chance and because she'd already paid the fees for it.

Our activity of choice the next year was gymnastics, with classes held in the gymnasium of the YMCA several suburbs away. Nine-year-old Cecelia was a wiry, bone-quick rocket of a runner, with a natural talent only gently nudged by the odd season at Little Athletics. I, on the other hand, was a slightly pot-bellied little seven-year-old. Despite my sister's sportiness, neither of us was particularly well coordinated, so the choice of gymnastics was truly baffling.

'Black kids don't do *gymnastics*!' my father spluttered, laughing, when Mum announced she had enrolled us.

This is how it happened, or else what's a story for?

Every Wednesday afternoon, my mother and little brother would pick us up from school and we'd drive to a quiet back street near the YMCA. We'd wolf down an afternoon snack in the car before undressing in the back seat of our enormous Ford Falcon, contorting our bodies into pastel-coloured leotards.

Maxine Beneba Clarke

At four o'clock, kids would file into the gym and assemble themselves by class level. We'd stand, my beginners' group, just as we'd been taught, ten or so small girls in assorted eighties-cut leotards, toes touching the white line across the auditorium floor.

Our instructor, a no-nonsense fifty-something redhead of German extraction, would start by inspecting our 'first positions'.

'Toes out, gerlz, heels touching!' She'd walk behind us wielding a table-tennis paddle she'd borrowed from the recreation room upstairs.

'Bottom een, Maczeen,' she'd remind me, tapping the paddle lightly on my behind.

I'd thrust my pelvis forward and will my bottom cheeks to somehow collapse in on themselves.

'Bottom eeen, sweetie, bottom eeen,' the teacher would entreat, waiting for me to obey her instruction, as my fellow junior gymnasts tittered in their perfectly buttock-tucked penguin stances. It wasn't just first to fifth position in which I encountered this problem. My rounded backside stopped me from properly holding myself up on the bars. It jutted out conspicuously at the instructor's eye level as I teetered on the balance beam. My offending behind was prodded with the toe of her pink and white Apple Pie sandshoe as I somersaulted across the mat.

'Tuck it, Maczeen,' she'd urge in frustration. 'Tuck ze thing eeen!'

It was as if she thought I was deliberately refusing to heed her instruction out of contempt for her authority. I had nothing against gymnastics, though it was clear I'd never be much good at it. Cartwheeling and somersaulting across the gym were fairly inoffensive activities, but because of the gym teacher's constant references to my physique, I began to dread Wednesday afternoons.

My mother, after sitting watching the first few weeks of classes, took the rare opportunity to have a coffee and a chat with one of the other mothers while classes were going on. I considered complaining to her, but was worried that she'd think it was merely a ploy to escape further classes. In any case, I was reluctant to alert anyone else – even other family members – to my deformity. There was something different, something protruding and sticky-outty and not-quite-right about my behind. I was sure that, in time, *everybody* would look at my body and realise that I was some kind of circus freak: the only little girl on earth whose bottom did not align neatly with her thighs when standing in first position. When news of my enormous bottom went public, I would probably need some kind of painful, humiliating bottom-trimming operation.

———————

As the term progressed, I started thinking about gymnastics class more and more. At school, the smell of chalk dust brought me back to the chalk pit in the gymnasium, where we dusted our hands for grip before working out on the double bars. The scent distracted me from my schoolwork. I could hear my gymnastics coach every moment of the school day, standing behind me, hissing, *Tuck ze thing eeen, Maczeeen. Tuck it eeen!*

I would lie in bed on Wednesday mornings constructing elaborate excuses to escape gymnastics class.

'Mum, I'm not feeling well,' I'd say, clutching at my stomach, hunched into foetal position.

'That's a shame,' Mum would reply, peeling the bedsheets from my body. 'I guess you won't be wanting any of the French toast I've cooked for you.'

I'd inevitably be full-bellied and halfway into my school uniform before I realised my mistake.

'I don't want to go to gymnastics anymore!' I wailed miserably one morning.

'Why not?' Mum sat down on the bed.

'My bottom!' I wailed.

'Oh.' Mum clearly wasn't sure what to make of this. 'Is it itchy?'

'No!' I said indignantly. 'I don't mean *worms*! I DON'T HAVE WORMS!'

My sister lifted her head from her pillow to see what the commotion was about.

My mother raised an eyebrow and glanced over at Cecelia in a *what-the-hell-is-going-on* kind of way.

'The gym coach keeps telling me to pull my bum in all the time. Only I can't.'

Mum looked at me, her nostrils flaring the way they did when she was trying to pretend something was serious but actually found it funny.

'Is that true?'

'Yes,' I howled, mortified. 'It's not *funny*.'

'Sorry to break it to you, but you do have a chubby bottom,' came the observation from my sister.

'Cecelia!' my mother warned sternly, before turning back to me.

'There's something wrong with me!' I sobbed.

'You have a very nice bottom,' my mother said, trying not to chuckle. '*I* gave that bottom to you and there's absolutely nothing wrong with it. Is there, Cecelia?' she asked pointedly.

'Nope.' My sister was sitting up in bed now, having realised she wasn't going to get any peace and quiet until the conversation had fully played out. 'But, then, I happen to think fat bottoms look really good.'

My mother looked daggers at her. 'I'll talk to the gym teacher. Now get up and get dressed or you'll be late for school.'

'No!' I grabbed Mum's hand. 'You can't talk to the teacher. Not about my *bottom*!' I couldn't believe Mum had even suggested such a thing. Obviously that would be even more humiliating than having my sticky-outty bottom slapped with a table tennis paddle every week for refusing to be tucked in.

'Well, what do you want me to do about it then?' Mum asked.

'Nothing!' Clearly there was no point asking my mother to help me alter my physical appearance. She actually thought there was nothing *wrong* with my behind, that it was *nice*.

'I hate gymnastics anyway. I don't want to go back.' I stuck my bottom lip out in a resolute pout.

'You don't have to go back next term if you don't want to', Mum said. 'There are still six weeks left this term, though, and you have to go because I've already paid for your lessons. Besides, I have to take Cecelia anyway.'

Six weeks. There was no way I'd be able to put up with *bottom in* for that much longer. Grumpily, I climbed out of bed and headed for the bathroom. I was going to have to come up with something on my own.

———————

The coach stood at one end of the room as we somersaulted a warm-up across the thin blue mats laid out end to end in the gymnasium. Her arms were folded proudly across her chest like a queen surveying her kingdom.

'Okay, girls!'

Maxine Beneba Clarke

We had finished tumbling and were waiting for her to join us at the far side of the gym. Head spinning, frizzy strands of hair escaping from my stumpy ponytail, I stood up as tall and straight as I could, sucking my stomach in underneath my rib cage.

'Positions!' she yelled, walking towards us.

We lined up, standing straight and tall in first position. I took my place in the middle of the line of ten or so leotard-clad little girls. I hated standing in line like that; I felt conspicuous among the other mostly white girls with their long, straight ponytails and their flat bottoms. It was like that segment my little brother, Bronson, watched on *Sesame Street*, where there was a whole line of completely identical things, like nine red circles, and one blue diamond would be on the end. They would play this song that drew attention to the odd one out and how it didn't belong.

I held my breath as the coach walked slowly along the line behind us, inspecting the turnout of our feet and the shape of our spines. When she reached me, she stopped for a moment.

'Maczeen,' she barked. 'Where iz your leeyotard?'

I feigned surprise, looking down at my baggy shorts and oversized t-shirt; shrugged.

'It was in the wash. I'm really sorry.' I attempted to appear genuinely regretful.

The coach paused. The silence seemed to stretch for an eternity. 'Next week,' she ordered, 'you wear ze leeyotard.' And off she moved, down the line.

I stood stock still with my heels together, toes pointing outwards, concentrating on my balance.

'*Okaaay!*' The coach had reached the end of the formation. 'Next position, pleeze!'

No mention of my sticky-outty bottom. No instruction to pull my stomach in so my derriere wasn't so conspicuous. Either coach couldn't *see* my bottom because of the loose-fitting clothes, or she was so distracted by my attire that she'd completely forgotten about my untuckability problem.

I resolved to find my craft scissors as soon as we got home – to cut up my leotard, or maybe drop it down the side of my bed, amid the lint and fluff and scrunched-up Minties wrappers, where my Mum's vacuum couldn't reach. I knew Mum wouldn't be buying me a replacement in a hurry if she found out it was lost. She'd definitely say shorts and t-shirts would have to suffice, and there would be no more *bottomz eeen* for me.

7.

THE POOR DOWNTRODDEN black people in the old American movies I saw as a child accepted their lot. They were always so good and God-fearing. They wore straw hats with flowers on them to Sunday church gatherings, and sat nodding their heads and clutching their bibles in the pews. They raised their gospel voices to praise the Lord when charismatic young preachers asked them to. When things went wrong, they prayed to Him to show them the way, knowing that He must have his reasons for even the most insurmountable of obstacles. The black characters in these movies were mostly servants and maids, who inexplicably found it in their gentle hearts to forgive the most sadistic white masters. They suffered unimaginable poverty, humiliation and torture. But in the end, somehow, someway, He always delivered them, even if through death, which was apparently also a gift from Him.

Even though we lived in a white middle-class area which would over the years gain notoriety as Sydney's evangelical Christian bible belt – home of the Hillsong megachurch – God did not venture into our family home on Hectare Street. My parents had both been exposed to religion in their early years:

were sporadically squeezed into spit-polished second-hand dress shoes and stiffly starched Sunday finery and dragged to church by their respective parents. These appearances at church had only been on special occasions – Easter and Christmas – and were rare enough to convey the message of being strictly insurance. Then, too, the concept of religion seemed amusing to my father, a mathematician who dealt in quantifiables.

I have only one memory of entering a church with my mother. In it, I am about four years old. We are walking, my mother and I, along Wrights Road on the way home from preschool, when the heavens unexpectedly open. Sheets of freezing rain pour down on us. Umbrella-less, we huddle under the small awning of the nearby white-painted timber Anglican church. But the rain seems to be chasing us, curving in under the church awning in piercing darts, as if directing us into the arms of the Lord.

When my mother eases open the heavy wooden church door, rows of polished wooden pews with plush red cushioning reveal themselves. Light streams through the pretty stained-glass windows.

'What is this place?' I am breathless with awe. 'It looks like the inside of a Pizza Hut restaurant!'

My mother shushes me. 'It's a church. People who believe in God come here to speak to him.'

We wait in silence until the downpour passes, then re-emerge onto the steamy rain-slicked street to continue our walk home.

When I was seven, though, I started praying to God almost every evening. Not because I actually thought he existed, but because there was one particular thing in the world I yearned for, and I thought it couldn't hurt to cover all bases.

One day, after months of murmuring hopefully into the darkness, He finally came through.

'Hold still for a moment,' my mother said.

It was around six o'clock on a weekday evening. We were standing, my parents and I, directly beneath the bathroom skylight, with the light also turned on. Mum tilted my face one way, then the next, as I fidgeted in my red-and-black school sports uniform. Dad stood in front of me in his collared work shirt and smart black trousers, his six-foot form hunched over as he stared down at my cheek.

'Mum! I can't see anything. The light's in my eyes!'

'There!' my mother said to my father, pointing to my right cheek.

Dad looked at my face closely, nodding as if not quite sure what he was supposed to be looking at, then grunted to himself and walked out of the bathroom. Mum looked my cheek over one more time for good measure.

'I am *beautiful*,' I stated matter-of-factly, trying to convince myself that this must be what all the fuss was about.

'Of course you are,' my mother said.

'Yeah. Beautifully ugly.' My sister appeared in the bathroom doorway, chuckling to herself as she caught the tail end of the conversation.

'*Cecelia*,' my mother reprimanded her half-heartedly as she put the plug in the bath and turned on the hot tap.

'Bags first bath!' I shouted. 'Can I have a bubble bath?'

'No. I think I'm going to put some olive oil in the bath. It's better for your skin.' My mother straightened up and looked at me thoughtfully.

'Yuck! I'm not having a greasy bath. That's totally foul.' Cecelia flounced off to our reluctantly shared bedroom.

My mother went to look for my little brother, and I undressed and got into the tub. Mum returned and lowered chubby Buddha-like Bronson into the warm bath as I trailed swirly patterns in the yellow oil pooled on the water's surface. It was my new beauty regime, I fantasised. The metamorphosis was starting; the ugly duckling becoming a swan. There'd be photographs and appearances in magazines and Target catalogues. I was blossoming into a stunning beauty.

I looked at Bronson, who was scooping up the oily bath water in a bright green kiddie cup and guzzling it down with great gusto. I smiled the most beautiful, widest smile I could muster. The modelling practice wasn't wasted on my little brother, who offered me a sip of oily water.

Later that evening, as I brushed my teeth, I stared closely at myself in the bathroom mirror. It was then that I noticed what Mum and Dad had been talking about. He – God – had answered my prayers.

Usually my skin was the exact colour of the coffee my father drank before work in the mornings. But in that moment, my face looked like my father's coffee when he'd just splashed a little cream on top of the bitter-smelling drink, and hadn't yet stirred. There was a lighter tan patch, right in the middle of my cheek. It was happening. *I was turning white.* I ran my hand over my cheek in excitement.

My elation was closely followed by pangs of guilt. No wonder my parents had seemed a bit worried. Soon, my life would be easier than theirs. Soon, I would be looking at them from the *other side*, where stares on the street and nasty remarks in grocery stores weren't commonplace. Where bandaids blended in, where hair worked *with* gravity, where underwear fit just the way it was supposed to.

I'd known somehow, when I prayed for this miracle, that there was something distinctly shameful about wanting to be something I could never be, something shameful about wanting to alter the colour of my skin – to be white. But it wasn't about wanting to be *better*. I didn't *dislike* being black. I didn't think being white would make me a better person. I just wanted to be like everyone else I knew, and everyone else mostly did not look like me.

Several weeks later, Mum sat twiddling her thumbs nervously as the two of us braved the eerie silence of the local dermatologist's office. The doctor, a grey-haired man in his mid-sixties inexplicably wearing a daggy purple bowtie over his crumpled white shirt, shone his penlight onto my cheeks, swivelled his chair away from us, and took a thick medical reference book from a shelf above his desk.

I looked around the office. There was a remote-controlled chair, with lots of lights above it; a cabinet holding bottles of cream. *Creams which might fix me*, I thought to myself. *Creams which might stop be from becoming white.* I might have known my parents would try to take this away from me. That no matter how often they'd told me over the years that skin colour didn't matter, having a *white* child simply wasn't part of their plan.

'Well, Mrs Clarke,' the doctor said, turning towards my mother, straight-backed and serious, 'do you mind if we have a little chat, just you and me? Maybe Maxine would like to sit in the waiting room. There are some really good books out there to read, and some colouring-in things.' He smiled widely as he stood, walked to his office door and opened it for me. There was something behind that smile, though – some kind of pity in his gaze.

'No. I'm staying here.' I hung my hands defiantly over the armrests of the chair and flopped back into it, unmoving.

'Can she stay here?' my mother asked uncertainly.

'Um, Mrs Clarke, I think it would be better if . . .'

My mother's face tightened. She fished around in her handbag. My mother's worn black leather handbag was like an Inspector Gadget accessory in its all-purpose usefulness, and like Doctor Who's TARDIS in capacity. At any given moment, Mum could rummage around in it to retrieve a foil-wrapped sandwich; a ChapStick; some Panadol or a packet of wet wipes. I never actually saw her put anything into her bag, yet whatever was called for always seemed to be hidden in its depths. That afternoon at the doctor's, her hand emerged clutching my latest half-read Baby-Sitters Club book. I got up from the chair, took the book from her, and walked out of the room.

———————————

My mother was quiet as we walked from the surgery to the car, looking straight ahead as I slurped deliberately loudly on the lollipop I'd taken from the jar on the reception counter.

'You see how there are some lighter patches on your face?' Mum eased the car out of the parking space.

I stared out the back window, moving the lollipop around my mouth, crashing it against my teeth. The streets of Baulkham Hills fell away outside the window: double-bricked, double-garaged and double-storeyed.

'I don't want you to worry about the way you look. The doctor said it could be nothing: just your skin stretching because you're growing a lot at the moment.' Mum sounded teary. 'I'm sure it will even out over the next few months.'

We stopped at a traffic light. Mum smiled reassuringly. 'There's nothing much we can do, just keep you out of the sun. Make sure you wear your school hat in the playground from now on, okay?'

———————

My sister snored loudly across the room. My brother babbled to himself as he jumped up and down in his cot in the bedroom next door in an effort to defy sleep. My mother was washing up in the kitchen: metal on metal sounding as she tumbled handfuls of rinsed cutlery onto the draining board. The front door opened, then closed quietly. My father's leather briefcase hit the wooden floorboards. My mother's feet padded towards him.

'How did it go?'

'Alright.'

There was a long silence. I imagined them, standing by the front door staring at each other. I was sad for them, because I was quite sure the doctor had told them there was nothing either of them could do. My prayers had been answered, and my parents were no match for Him. I would become white, no matter what they did – regardless of how hard they tried to stop me slipping away from them.

'There's not much we can do . . . It will probably even out . . . This is the worst-case scenario.'

The sound of paper rustling.

'Jesus, Cleo. Is she really going to look like that?'

'Worst-case scenario, he said.' More page-turning.

70

'Worst-case scenario? What does that bloody mean?'

'Calm down, Bordy. I'm sure it will sort itself out.'

'Vitiligo! Isn't that what Michael Jackson—'

'Jesus, Bordeaux! You are *not* helping!'

My parents lowered their voices.

'It might not be that. They can't be sure.' My mother's prag-matic tone.

'They couldn't suggest anything else, though?' My father's practical one. 'Jesus Christ. Look at these pictures.'

'I know, I know, I know,' repeated Mum. 'Let's not even look at them.'

I heard the door of the cabinet in the lounge room open and shut, and then their voices faded as my parents moved to the other side of the house.

Outside, on Hectare Street, the traffic slowed. Cecelia rolled over in her bed. I quietly peeled back my sheets, and walked down the hallway and into the lounge room. The curtains were wide open. Streetlight bathed the room. The cabinet door opened easily. I reached in and removed the brochures.

Vitiligo, the pamphlet was headed. I sounded the word out. It hovered on my tongue, finally stumbling out in staccato syllables.

'*Vitiligo is a pig . . . pig-mentation disorder caused by loss of pig . . . pig-ment in the skin. As a result of this loss of pigment, white patches form . . .*' My eyes were suddenly drawn to the photographs. At various intervals throughout the medical pamphlet were glum-looking otherworldly people whose skin was marbled pink and brown. Their skin looked like *actual marble* – the white patches slowly spreading over their dark skin like flat light-pinkish birthmarks. According to the pamphlet, vitiligo was a skin disease – and from what my parents had said, it was about to spread all over me. The marbled people seemed, to my young eyes, to be brown people in varying stages of becoming white.

I was right. My prayers *had* been answered. Eventually the light brown patches on my face would turn pink. Eventually that pinkness would creep around the rest of my body. Eventually, I was certain, I would emerge from the vitiligo *white*: free from golliwog jokes, 'bad' hair and my untuckable bottom. Cecelia would be so jealous of me! I couldn't wait to see the look on her face when she found out. I wouldn't be banned from playmates' houses because their parents considered me a *bad influence*. Carlita Allen would leave me alone. I quickly replaced the brochures in the cabinet and crept back to bed, elated.

On the surface of my skin, a miracle was quietly brewing.

8.

I WAITED MONTHS for the light patches on my face to lighten and spread – for the edges of the whitish-beige splotches to melt into each other until I was covered all over in the lighter pigment. I was sure my brown colouring would then wash out all together into the pinkish off-white complexion of the other kids in my class. But no matter how much I secretly prayed to Him to expedite the process, the inconsistencies in my skin remained stagnant, giving my face the appearance of being slightly watermarked.

I was accustomed already to various schoolyard slurs in relation to my skin colour. *Blackie*; *golliwog*; *turd* – these throwaway jeers would accompany me throughout my school life. When I complained to my parents, their outraged complaints to school management resulted in lukewarm reprimands to the bullies in question, after which the taunting would immediately escalate. But now the vitiligo became another source of harassment.

'What's wrong with your face?' a boy in the other grade two class asked loudly as we lined up to play tunnel ball. 'You look like my dog. He's got white and brown patches all over him too. His name is Patch.'

Laughter rippled along the line. The parent helper for our gross motor skills session that morning looked at me with pity, but offered neither reprimand or support. I looked away, pretending to ignore the comment, shuffled my feet into position at the back end of the tunnel ball crush. Heat rose in my cheeks as I turned around and bent to look through the tunnel of grass-stained socks and sunburnt legs. The worn orange basketball slipped through my fingers and rolled towards the back of the concrete tennis court.

'Go get the ball, Patch! Go fetch!' a girl's shrill voice rang out.

'Yeah! Fetch, Patch! Go fetch, doggy!'

'Fetch, girl, fetch!'

The other tunnel ballers collapsed with giggles. I walked stiffly after the ball. My eyes welled up with tears. If there really was a God, He hated me. I wanted to disappear. To *not be.* My breathing grew shallow; my sight blurry. My bones ached, like when I'd had the flu. I felt like I was free-falling through space. I wanted out, to not exist anymore.

———

At home, my mother started applying her own liquid foundation to my face each morning before school. I'd stand in front of the mirror as she poured what looked like melted chocolate from a small glass bottle onto balls of cotton wool, and carefully dabbed it all over my face to even out my complexion.

This temporary solution brought its own unique problems: on sports days, or under the sun, the make-up mixed with perspiration and ran down my chin to form grubby brown patches on my uniform collar. The temptation to scratch, pick my nose or rest my chin on my hand when tired meant that the foundation also transferred to my hands, which then left brown smudges on my workbooks, my cheese-and-lettuce sandwiches and almost everything else I touched. Now I wasn't just brown and strange-looking, I was also *dirty*.

'Oh, Maxine,' the school librarian sighed, as she looked at the brown streaks on my library borrowing card. 'How do you get everything so grubby?'

'I don't know.'

'Did you wash your hands before you picked up the library book? You need to *wash your hands*.'

'I did wash my hands.'

'She can't help it. She's just *dirty*.' One of the other kids giggled.

Another of my classmates made a vomiting noise.

The name Patch stuck. So much so that I wished the other awful names would come back. Golliwog, which was what they called me after Allison brought in her favourite doll for show-and-tell: the little coal-black stuffed toy with wide white eyes, a shock of black woollen hair and a garish bright red mouth. Gorilla Girl, which was often accompanied by chimpanzee noises, and which had started when a boy in my class wiped squashed banana on my back as I was eating my lunch. I didn't care which of those they called me now – just as long as it wasn't the name of a dog.

'You're so *sensitive*, Maxine,' the playground duty teacher would say when I complained. 'Just ignore them darling, okay?'

I learned to stay quiet. I learned that nobody much cared. I learned that it was probably my fault anyway, and that what they were doing to me was perfectly okay. This is how it alters us. This is how we change.

Maxine Beneba Clarke

Under the fierce heat of an Australian January, the light sections of my skin began to regain their pigment. By the time school resumed in early February, my complexion had evened out enough not to warrant the daily application of foundation. One part of me was bitterly disappointed, but the other was elated. I understood, by then, that the pigment inconsistencies were the result of a skin disease. That I would *always* be a little brown girl, and after that, a brown woman. This reality made me feel tired, right down to my bones.

These were the blues that wailed over me. Hear my story, sing.

There was one facet of my graduation to grade two which I'd been simultaneously apprehensive and excited about. Being in grade two at my primary school meant gaining entry to the dubious world of Catch and Kiss. Catch and Kiss was a game the infants school teachers were continually trying to ban. Mrs Gerard, my grade two teacher and the head of the infants school, was a willowy grandmotherly type who wore white cotton blouses with large shoulder pads in them, pearl brooches, tailored skirts down to her calves, and daggy tan stockings which always wrinkled and sagged around her ankles by the end of the school day.

Mrs Gerard was so horrified at the thought of seven- and eight-year-old children engaging in physical affection with members of the opposite sex that she couldn't even bear to name the game. She preferred, instead, to refer to Catch and Kiss at Monday morning assembly as *That Running Game You Older Children Play*.

After the national anthem was finished and we were seated cross-legged in the school hall, merit awards were handed out to students from each class. Mrs Gerard would then run through the reprimands for the week.

'Let me remind you again,' she'd finish, peering through her spectacles towards the back of the hall, where the grade two children were seated, 'any child caught playing *That Running Game You Older Children Play* will be very swiftly dealt with.'

A titter would move through the hall. Every kid from kindergarten to grade two knew that no matter what the teachers said or did, the ban on Catch and Kiss would remain ineffective. Catch and Kissers employed various deceptions to avoid detection. Some lunchtimes, one child would be allocated to tail the playground duty teacher, shouting a pre-agreed warning – like *paddle pop* or *jump rope* – when the duty teacher drew close. Then, too, there was no way for the teachers to definitively prove what we were doing, and those unfortunate enough to fall under suspicion knew better than to cave under interrogation.

'Did you just kiss Allison?' the duty teacher would ask, rounding the corner suddenly.

'No.' The boy in question would look at the teacher indignantly.

'What were you doing then?'

'I was running and I accidentally bumped into her.'

'Is that the truth, Allison?' The duty teacher would always appeal to the conscience of kids they figured were more likely to slip up.

'His mouth fell on my cheek.'

'Are you sure that's true? I think you were playing Catch and Kiss.'

'No, miss. I mean, yes, miss – I mean, I *wasn't* playing it.'

The top half of the infants playground was the area designated for Catch and Kiss. The concrete hut containing a row of low-set drinking bubblers was the designated B.A.R. tag-safe starting point. The large gum tree on the border of the infants and primary playgrounds was the finishing point, and also B.A.R., which meant you couldn't be caught or kissed while you were touching it. These three letters were pronounced separately, sounded out with great reverence, though none of us knew what B.A.R. actually stood for.

The mission for us girls, in order to win the game of Catch and Kiss, was to gather inside the bubbler hut, then make the sixty-metre dash to the gum tree, dodging the clumsy, knobbly-kneed seven-year-old boys who stationed themselves between B.A.R.s with the aim of smacking their peanut-buttery lips on our cheeks. Once kissed, you were *out*, and had to sit down where you'd been accosted until the game was over and there were no more runners to be kissed. After each dash, the remaining girls about-faced and began the return journey, until there was only one un-kissed girl victor.

I found myself to be a champion at Catch and Kiss, despite being a slow runner. Little Athletics was our family's extracurricular activity for the term, on account of my sister having a gift for athletics, and the fact that it was on a Saturday, which meant my father was able to take us and my mother could have a break. At Little Athletics, having a track-star sister had roused a flurry of expectation. The designated coach for the Under 8s would stare on perplexed as I puffed, wheezed and complained my way to each finish line, straggling behind the rest of the group: black bloomers cutting into my chubby thighs, wisps of wild afro escaping from the small powder-puff ponytail on top of my head.

For some reason, Catch and Kiss was a completely different story. I'd stand in the bubbler hut the moment before the chase, front knee bent like the sprinters in the athletics championships on television. I'd focus my gaze straight in front of me, staring through the mass of seven-year-old boys until I'd mapped a crooked path through the catchers. When I heard the word *go* screamed out by the designated starter, it was as if the whole world moved in slow motion.

There was a woman my father liked to watch in the athletics championships on our small television. When Dad knew she was coming on, he'd get out of his armchair and adjust the silver dial, clicking through all the potential reception channels until he found the clearest picture possible. Flo Jo, African American sprinter Florence Griffith Joyner, had chocolate brown skin, wavy jet-black hair, and long fingernails which she painted silver, or blood orange, or red, white and blue, like the American flag. We couldn't see the colours on our black-and-white telly, but I'd seen them in the pages of the women's magazines in our local doctor's surgery. Even when sprinting, Flo Jo wore bright red lipstick. Crimson rouge accentuated her high, proud cheekbones. Flo Jo was one of the fastest women on earth, yet she was graceful and stunning, and never seemed to break a sweat.

When I was bolting from B.A.R. to B.A.R. at the top of the infants playground, I was just like Flo Jo. I felt I was the speediest girl on the planet. *If you want it bad enough, just take it!* I could imagine one of Flo Jo's impromptu end-of-race speeches in my ears as my feet thudded across the grass. *Use everything you've got – you can rest at the end.* That was the kind of thing Flo Jo would say when the sports commentators asked her what she'd been thinking about while she was running. I was just like her, fast as lightning, some kind of sparkly black magic. The boys were forced to eat my dust as I ducked and swerved out of their reach.

A month or so after commencing Catch and Kiss at lunchtime, I stood sheltering in B.A.R., with twenty or so boys lined up

79

between myself and the large gum tree. Sitting dotted around on the grass were most of the girls from our grade. Carlita, Kelly and Sara, who always got caught out in the first few minutes of the game, sat in a blonde cross-legged huddle, making daisy chains and swapping lip glosses. Further down sat the smart clique: Emma, Jane and Jennifer, who were always caught by the more studious boys in the class. They were playing a clapping game, their palms slapping and connecting to the rhythm of their singsong melody. I looked around the bubbler hut. The only girls still in the game were myself; Belinda, who still had what Mrs Gerard called *serious toileting issues* and perpetually smelled like the wee smell that drifted out of the boys toilets; Mahana, the light brown girl who had recently started at our school with her twin brother Amir, and who wasn't allowed to eat ham or sit in scripture classes or talk to boys; and Claire, the grade two bossy-boots.

I'd been the victor of Catch and Kiss for the last few days, but suddenly winning didn't seem like such a victory.

'Go!' shouted one of the boys.

Belinda, Claire and I made a run for it. Only this time, I didn't try to pick a path through the scrum. I made a beeline straight for Lewis Stevens. If anybody was going to kiss me, I wanted it to be Lewis. Lewis had straight dark brown hair and a cute smattering of freckles across his nose. He was the smartest kid in our class, and had pipped me at the post every year so far for the class academic award on awards night. Lewis always got his spelling words right, and could read and write as well as me, which was highly unusual. To cap it all off, Lewis Stevens was *nice*. He had never teased me about my brownness. Even though he never said anything in my defence, he always looked very uncomfortable when Carlita or anyone else started hassling me.

I fixed my eyes on Lewis's grey school shirt and high-waisted shorts, and swerved until I was directly near him. Lewis opened his eyes wide in surprise. He stepped to the side. I sidestepped with him, leaned my face in and waited for him to plant a kiss on my eager cheek. Another boy came running up behind Lewis and pushed Lewis's face forward. Lewis's cheek against mine was warm and soft.

'I'm out! I'm out! I got kissed!' I whooped, and promptly sat down on the grass.

'Errrrrr! Lewis kissed the Golliwog! Lewis kissed Patch! He is gonna get her *disease*!'

'That's disgusting!'

'Nobody go near Lewis – he's contagious now!'

'She put her dirty face on him! Eeeeew!'

'Lewis and Patch are gonna have ugly dog-babies together!'

The playground erupted into a chorus of disgusted squeals. Lewis looked down at me, his face red with anger and hurt. I hated the way he was staring at me: as if I'd turned on him, as if I'd somehow betrayed him. He turned on his heel and strode off down the other end of the playground. I stared down at the grass, devastated.

I wasn't, after all, the speed demon I had imagined myself to be. It was just that nobody wanted to touch me, let alone kiss me. The truth was, in the game of Catch and Kiss, it was the losers who really won. I jumped up from the grass and ran around the back of the bubbler huts and into the girls toilets.

In memories of my childhood, the inside walls of primary school toilet stalls press in on me. The paint is peeling. Sometimes swear words are scraped into the wall in a furtive, childish hand. The aluminium toilet bowl is smelly and stained. There is the loud trickle of hands being washed outside the stall: of water crashing into the metal sinks. There is the sporadic whirr of toilet roll holders as paper is pulled for wiping. In this filthy, smelly, uninhabitable place, there is the feeling of a safe haven: I find my breathing space.

9.

IN 1988, AUSTRALIA was coming off the back of several years of economic crisis. Race relations had begun to take a turn for the worse. John Howard, the leader of the Liberal opposition party, was openly antipathetic to multiculturalism, opposed to recognising Indigenous land rights and advocated slowing down immigration from Asia. Informed by the anti-immigration sentiment of England's Thatcher government, these policies together formed the founding principles of the Liberal–National Coalition's multiculturalism and ethnic affairs policy: One Australia.

Labor prime minister Bob Hawke condemned this new stance as a return to the fear and intolerance of the White Australia era, but in the political sphere, xenophobic rhetoric was gaining ground. The Australian Nationalist Movement, a neo-Nazi group with their headquarters in Perth, bill-posted against Asian immigration and openly harassed those they saw as a threat to their pro-white anti-immigration philosophy. These developments highlighted a sentiment which directly contradicted the kind of Australia Gough Whitlam had promoted at the time my parents first decided to migrate.

This was also the year of Australia's bicentenary celebrations, in which the country would commemorate the two-hundred-year anniversary of Governor Arthur Phillip's arrival in Australia with the First Fleet of eleven ships from England, founding the colony of New South Wales.

My athletics-mad father brought home a colour television set, in preparation for watching the 1988 Olympics, and the first thing we happened to see, once the television was connected and the aerial adjusted, was a re-enactment of the arrival of the First Fleet into Sydney Harbour. A parade of odd-looking tall ships slowly approached the docks, sails billowing. People swarmed the foreshore, cheering and waving small Australian flags with the red Union Jack and white stars of the Southern Cross prominent against the navy blue background.

In another news report that same evening, we saw footage of crowds of people walking across the Harbour Bridge. These people didn't seem elated, like the crowd that had welcomed the First Fleet re-enactment, though they too carried a flag. It was one I had seen before, on our black-and-white television: the flag that was held by the Aboriginal people when their big sacred rock, Uluru, was handed back to them. I could see now that the bottom half of the flag was red, the top half black, and the circle in the middle was yellow. The Aboriginal flag adorned the t-shirts, placards and badges of those marching. WHITE AUSTRALIA HAS A BLACK HISTORY one placard read. DON'T CELEBRATE 1988 read another. ALWAYS WAS, ALWAYS WILL BE, ABORIGINAL LAND. The crowd comprised people of all shapes, sizes and colours, and they were all yelling. It was a gathering like I'd never seen before in my life. I stood in the middle of the lounge room, staring at the scene unfolding on the TV screen.

'What are they doing?' I asked, fascinated.

'Protesting,' Mum said absent-mindedly from her ironing station in front of the balcony glass doors.

'What's protesting?'

'It's . . . well, it's when you stand up against something that you disagree with. When you *let it be known* you disagree with a thing.'

'What do those people on telly disagree with?'

My mother paused. 'They don't agree with celebrating the bicentenary.'

'Why not?'

'It's the anniversary of when Europeans came to this country.'

'What are Europeans?'

'People from Europe.' My mother cleared her throat. '*White people*. The people protesting don't believe the bicentenary should be celebrated, because it wasn't a nice time for Aboriginal people, the day white people came.'

'Why not?'

'It just wasn't,' Mum said.

I nodded knowingly. I knew a bit more about the Aborigines now that I was in grade three. In *Dot and the Kangaroo*, which we'd watched in the school hall one rainy lunchtime, the little red-headed girl and her kangaroo friend had sheltered in a cave. Inside the cave, there were pictures drawn on the wall by the Aborigines. The kangaroo had explained to Dot that tribespeople used to live in the cave, but a scary bunyip came out of the billabong and ate them. This was why there were no more Aboriginal tribespeople in the area, said the kangaroo: because the bunyip had scared them off. The protest march on telly was probably about the bunyips, I reasoned.

———————

At school, bicentenary celebrations were in full swing. We decorated our classroom with drawings of Governor Arthur Phillip, and made models of the First Fleet out of tissue paper, matchsticks and paddle-pop sticks. We talked about the difficult lives of the settlers, how they were *true pioneers*. Mrs Hird, our grade three teacher, always uttered the word *pioneers* with great reverence.

In our bicentenary lessons, we learned that the Aborigines were the brown people who were already in Australia when Cook discovered the country. The Aborigines hunted animals with boomerangs, did corroboree dances and ate grubs, our teacher told us.

'How could Captain Cook discover Australia if there were already people here?' I asked Mrs Hird dubiously.

'He discovered it, because nobody knew it existed,' Mrs Hird explained patiently. 'Nobody had been to Australia before he arrived here as an explorer.' She returned to writing on the blackboard, as if what she said had made perfect sense.

'But, Mrs Hird, if the Aborigines were *already* here—'

'They're . . . they're *different*. Only *they* knew they were here.'

I stared at my teacher, perplexed, as she continued writing the Explorers' Timeline.

———————

After school one day, Mum lined up our three red schoolbags on the kitchen surface, unpacked our lunchboxes and drink bottles, and fished our homework books out of our bags. 'What's this?' She was holding up Cecelia's open workbook.

In the centre of the page was a drawing, with a caption carefully written underneath.

'That's mine.' Cecelia looked up from the kitchen table, where she, Bronson and I were all busy slathering butter and honey onto pikelets. 'I did it in class today.'

'Did you draw it by yourself?'

'No.' My sister shrugged. 'I traced it from a book at school.'

'Did you copy the writing, or did you make it up yourself?'

'I copied it from the book.'

Mum stared at the picture for a moment, then put the workbook on the kitchen counter, still open, and went on unpacking our schoolbags. I got up from my seat and moved over to look at the picture. Captain Arthur Phillip stood in the centre of the sketch in straight-backed, uniformed glory. His navy blue hat perched majestically on his silver-grey curls. The gold trimmings on his dark coat were filled in with orange and yellow crayon flecks. On the edge of the page stood two loin-clothed Aboriginal men, their faces contorted into scowls. Each of them held a long spear in their right hand, poised to throw at the amiable-looking Captain Phillip. Written underneath the picture, in my sister's handwriting, was the caption: *Captain Phillip tried hard to be friendly, but the Aborigines were violent and hostile.*

A fortnightly treat for us kids was our visit to one of the local public libraries: either the Baulkham Hills library, off Windsor Road, near the infamous Bull and Bush Hotel, or the Castle Hill library, nestled among the restaurants and shops in the main shopping strip on Old Northern Road. We were such frequent visitors that the libraries knew our borrowing habits inside out.

4

Maxine Beneba Clarke

'Hello, are you looking for more Baby-Sitters Little Sister books? I think most of them are out this week,' the kindly librarian volunteered when she saw me.

'No, I'm looking for something else.' I quickly slammed the wooden drawer of the card catalogue shut.

'Maybe I can help you?'

'Maybe.' I looked at her uncertainly, weighing up the possibility of finding the information I was after on my own.

'What are you looking for?'

'I don't really know,' I said with a shrug.

'You don't know the name of the book? Maybe you can describe it to me.'

I ground one toe of my sneaker into the carpet. 'We're learning about the First Fleet in class. I want to borrow a book about that.'

'Oh.' She sounded surprised. 'Well aren't you a studious little girl! I'm sure I can find something for you.'

'Thanks.' I didn't know what *studious* meant, but it sounded like it was a good thing. 'Maybe you could, um, also please find me something about the Aborigines,' I added, as casually as I could. 'Please.'

'Of course.' She didn't bat an eyelid.

The librarian pulled out three cards from the catalogue and wandered over to the back section of the library. I followed her closely, keeping one eye on Mum, who was over in the picture book section choosing books with Bronson. The lady pulled two books from the adults borrowing shelves, then moved over to the section where the kids' history books were, adding another book to the small pile.

'Here you are. Two of these books are for grown-ups, but I'm sure your mum will be able to help you read them. Just check

88

with her first before you borrow them. The other one should be okay to read by yourself.' She bustled off to deal with a man standing impatiently at the borrowing counter.

With one eye on the librarian and the other still on my mother and siblings, I found a deserted aisle and sat down on a metal stool between the two rows of shelving. I opened the kids' history book. There were colourful pictures of Captain Cook and kangaroos sprinkled across the pages. It was the exact same book our teacher had been using in class. I put it on the floor at my feet and opened the red-covered book, peering through the gaps in the metal shelving to make sure nobody was coming. My mother was busy fending off Cecelia's protestations of boredom and trying to convince Bronson that *all* of the books he borrowed didn't need to have Ninja Turtles on the front cover.

In the centre of the red book was a photograph of eight Aboriginal men. They stood side by side, staring vacantly into the camera lens. They were emaciated: collarbones and knee bones jutting out, cheeks gaunt and sunken. Their eyes looked sorrowful, deadened. The black men were shackled together, a mere metre of chain separating each metal neck cuff.

On another page was a sketch of white men in broad-brimmed hats and buttoned blazers, riding bucking horses. They were slashing down a crowd of wailing Aboriginal people with long swords. The caption underneath the sketch read *Myall Creek Massacre*. My eyes widened. I stared at the bloody scene in shock.

'Didn't find what you were after then?' the librarian asked, as I checked out my usual mixture of Baby-Sitters and Judy Blume titles.

'I did, thanks. I just, um, didn't need to borrow it,' I mumbled into my pile of books.

'What's that?' my mother asked.

'Oh, she's a bright spark this one, wanted to do some research for school.'

My mother looked down at me doubtfully for a moment, then turned to run after Bronson, who was making a sly exit through the glass doors with a stack of Ninja Turtle books that hadn't been checked out yet.

———————

A major part of the school's bicentenary celebrations was Colonial Day. Each student would have to dress up in colonial wear: pyjama-style prison outfits like the convicts used to wear, smart blazers, jodhpurs and boots like those worn by the gentlemen of the colony, or the bonnets and long skirts preferred by the ladies of the era. Parents and community members would come to watch the Colonial Day parade. The school community would then be served a 'settlers morning tea' of tea and scones.

In the days leading up to the Colonial Day parade, the zip, whirr and thud of my mother's sewing machine could be heard late into the night as she fashioned long cream-and-blue-checked skirts and dainty lace-trimmed bonnets for my sister and me. My brother, who was now in kindergarten, would be wearing a revamped version of a soldiers outfit we already had in our dress-up box. Mum had bought gold-painted plastic buttons to replace the black ones on the smart red jacket. For trousers he'd wear navy tracksuit pants tucked into his long black gumboots.

I'd seen the look on Mum's face, though, when I'd taken the bright red note about the Colonial Day parade out of my school-bag: how she'd stood at the kitchen bench reading it, then set it down on the benchtop and held her breath in for just a moment.

'Mum?'

'Yes, darling?' Mum had to raise her voice above the whirr of the sewing machine, her eyes glued to the neat row of dark blue stitches.

'I don't want to go in the parade.'

Mum took her foot off the pedal. 'Why not?'

'I just don't.'

'I've almost finished your outfit.'

'I'm not wearing it.' I stuck my bottom lip out.

'Maxine, what's this about?'

'Nothing.' It wasn't nothing. It was everything. It was the photograph of those shackled brown men. It was the drawings I'd seen of those Aboriginal people being killed. It was the look on my mother's face when she'd seen the caption about Captain Phillip in my sister's workbook. It was Ayers Rock being Uluru. It was the stream of shouting people we'd seen snaking over the Harbour Bridge with their WHITE AUSTRALIA HAS A BLACK HISTORY signs. It was the bunyip. It was a deep, unsettling feeling I couldn't shake, but also couldn't properly articulate or understand.

Mum sighed, ripped a loose thread from the bonnet with her teeth, and got up from behind the sewing machine. She smoothed back the black frizz escaping from my ponytail, and put the bonnet on my head, tying the white ribbons into a bow under my chin. The hat felt stiff and awkward. The lace trimming scratched at my forehead as I tilted my head to look up at her.

On the day of the parade, three hundred primary school kids lined up in mock colonial costumes, divided into soldiers, convicts and settlers. Miniature aproned housewives wore impractical floor-length dresses which dragged behind us in the dry dirt.

Bronson and a gang of other boisterous kindergarten soldiers had to be coaxed away from a nest of stink bugs they'd discovered at the base of an enormous eucalypt tree down the back of the playground. The convicts went barefoot: dressed in white tracksuits with arrows drawn over them in permanent black marker. They scampered from the dry dirt to the scratchy grass and back again, hopping to avoid the angry bull ants the parade had stirred up.

We walked around the back playground in a lopsided circle, showing off our costumes to the parents and community members in attendance. At opportune moments, the little soldier boys would stop to whip out black-painted water pistols and aim them at the crowd.

I shuffled my feet around the oval: head down, bonnet low on my brow, staring at the soil beneath my polished black buckle-up shoes.

For the first time, I thought about the land beneath my feet; about who it belonged to, about the people who'd been here before me. I could remember something – some older children I had seen, *black* children, walking up Hectare Street where we lived, way back when I was in preschool. I remembered them looking over curiously then waving at me. This recollection came from somewhere deep in the recesses of my mind. But it couldn't be right. It seemed fuzzy to me, like some kind of dream.

It would be years – decades – before I would learn about Marella Mission Farm for Aboriginal children, just past the edge of Kellyville village. It would be years before I would learn that not two kilometres from our home, unbeknown to our family, had been living a houseful of 'removed' Aboriginal children.

But walking around the school grounds on the morning of the Colonial Day parade, I felt a kind of awe at knowing I was definitely on black country. Not my family's country of origin;

I knew by then that my parents had been born in a distant part of the world. But all the same I felt the knowledge of it – of the certain blackness of the country I was born in and raised on – fundamentally alter something inside me.

10.

MY FIRST TWO-WHEEL bike was a bright shiny candy red, like the glacé cherries Mum sometimes cooked into her bread pudding. The grips on the handlebars had been white when I'd first got the bike on my sixth birthday, but by the time I was eight years old, dirt and wear had scuffed them grey. Red and white plastic streamers dangled from the handlebars, as I fast-pedalled the sleek two-wheeler around the sleepy Kellyville streets.

Before the red bike, all of the scooters and tricycles I'd owned had been worn hand-me-downs, passed on from various family friends or my older sister, Cecelia.

There was a song I sang when I rode my red two-wheeler up and down our driveway, with my squarish white stackhat tightly fastened under my chin. I was in the school choir, and loved performing songs almost as much as I loved escaping the playground to the relative safety of singing practice every Wednesday lunchtime. But while the words in most of the songs we learned in choir − 'Waltzing Matilda', 'Home Among the Gum Trees', 'True Blue' − didn't make much sense to me, I knew exactly what my *bike song* was about.

I'd put my hands on the handlebars, swing one leg over the bike, and take a deep breath. I'd ride up one of the thin concrete tyre paths on our front driveway, around the carefully mowed strip of grass in the middle, make a narrow turn and cruise back up the other tyre path in an endless loop. On some laps, I sang my song out loud. On others, it rang out inside my head. I sang about the land spreading out before me, under the starry skies, I sang: 'Don't Fence Me In'. I sang about gazing up at the round yellow moon until I lost my senses. 'Don't fence me in,' I begged, 'please don't fence me in.' The freedom of movement – the rush of riding – was addictive.

I outgrew my red bike around the same time Bronson grew too big for the tiny BMX bike we'd found on the roadside on an evening stroll. Dad undertook to build us both 'new' bikes, instead of buying them from a shop.

My father had been enrolled in electrical engineering at university before transferring to pure mathematics. The love of building things and making things go had never left him.

Dad was dedicated to music in the same way he obsessed over numbers. Cubes of record-shelving covered one entire wall of our lounge room, from ceiling to floor. Dad had collected records and audio equipment since he was a teenager. His records were kept in impeccable condition, and woe betide the entire household if Dad walked past his records and found the spines uneven or the titles out of alphabetic order. He tinkered incessantly with the stereo and its two massive speakers. He'd also take apart anything else in the house that was broken – the air conditioners, the kitchen fan, one of Bronson's remote control cars. He would immediately be able to identify the problem – a broken circuit, a loose or corroded wire – and would poke about with a wrench or screwdriver or pliers or drill until whatever was ailing had been righted again.

Thus, Dad's offer to build Bronson and I new bikes was nothing out of the ordinary. He would disappear off to the salvage section of the local tip on weekends and return with various combinations of frames and handlebars, or come home with cans of spray paint from the local hardware store or tyres and bells from the bike shop.

Eventually, two beautiful new bikes stood in the front driveway. Mine was painted a sparkly green, blinged up with light green thick-tread wheels and an enormous silver bell. The handlebars scooped downwards in the middle into a deep U shape, like the handlebars of a Harley Davidson motorcycle. It looked like the kind of bike Winnie rode on *The Wonder Years*. I fell in love with it at first sight. Bronson's bike was spray-painted sparkly gold and fitted out with heavy-tread yellow wheels. There was a movie that was often rerun on television during the school holidays, called *BMX Bandits*. It was about a group of kids who were awesome BMX riders. The brightly coloured thick-tread wheels on our new bikes reminded me of this movie, and of the beautiful, daring strawberry-blonde girl who starred in it. I was – *we were* – going to have great adventures on these bikes, just like the BMX bandits. Perhaps we, too, would foil robberies and become local heroes. Even if we didn't, these bikes my father had somehow magicked up out of nothing would mark the beginning of an amazing summer.

Around the corner from our house was a large children's playground. The playground equipment was woeful – two swings and a sad-looking climbing frame. There was hardly ever anyone playing on it. The main attraction was the BMX track which wound its way around and over six large artificial hills. It was lined with gravel sharp enough to cause nasty scrapes when we stacked it, but loosely packed enough to create a blinding dust storm when we skidded to a stop.

The largest hill at the Kellyville BMX track was a veritable mountain: almost insurmountable. I would bump over the dirt and gravel of the smaller hills, gradually making my way towards the base of the large hill. I would pedal for all I was worth, huffing and puffing, my thighs aching from the strain. But when I reached the top of the big hill, I would stop, climb off my bike, and walk to the bottom. Then I'd remount the bike and keep riding around the track. Each time I got to the top of the big hill, I'd will myself to ride down it – to be brave enough, to be the BMX bandit I knew I could be. But I could never quite manage it. On this new bike, though, I was certain things would be different.

Bronson and I arranged to meet some local kids at the BMX track. By a stroke of luck, the McGuires also had two older girls and a younger boy the same ages as my brother, sister and me.

When Bronson and I reached the park, we waited at the kerb until we saw the two youngest McGuire kids, Jennifer and Nathan, walking up the steep incline of their street towards the park, wheeling their bikes in front of them.

'Awesome!'

'Look at your bikes!'

'Our Dad *built* them for us!' I told them proudly.

The four of us headed towards the BMX track, Bronson at the front of the pack, wearing his purple Hypercolor t-shirt, which was already turning pink across the back. We wheeled our bikes up to the top of a medium-sized hill. I waited until the three others had taken off, then coasted to the bottom. Pedal-pedal-pedal. My bike hovered at the top of the second hill. Once again, I let myself fly down the other side. Pedal-pedal-pedal-pedal. The bike hovered for a fraction of a second at the top of the next hill.

'Your bikes look so cool!' Jennifer yelled. 'They go so fast.'

It *felt* like we were going faster than we had on our old bikes. The heavy-tread wheels were perfect for the bike track. My green bike didn't skitter and skid like my little red beauty had on its thin tyres. When I got to the top of the biggest hill, where Jennifer was waiting, I pedalled right past her without a second thought, flying down at a speed I'd never reached before.

'Auuuuuugh!' I screamed in delight. 'I did it! I went down!' I felt on top of the world.

Bronson, Jennifer and Nathan whooped and cheered. The momentum propelled me up the next hill, where I put my feet to the ground and skidded to a stop. Over by the road, making their way into the park, I could see a group of kids, four or five of them, all boys, all on their bikes. One of them raised a finger and pointed in our direction. I stopped and waited for Bronson and the McGuire kids to catch up to me, then gestured to the approaching kids.

'Let's just keep riding,' Jennifer suggested.

By the time we made our way around the course again and back up to the top of the big hill, the boys had reached the opposite side of the track.

'Oi! Blackies! Nice bikes. Where'd you get them from? The Reject Shop? Get off our track!' one of them yelled.

The other kids in the group laughed.

'Get lost!' yelled my little brother, into the wind.

'We said get off the track, blackies!' another of the boys yelled.
'With your *loser* bikes.'

I suddenly recognised the kid. He was in my class at school
and lived on the same street as the McGuires.

'We said no!' Bronson yelled again, defiant.

'Maybe we should go home?' suggested Jennifer nervously.

Bronson looked at her, then at Nathan, frustration flashing
across his face. He was small for his age, my brother. As a baby
he'd arrived six weeks early, his lungs underdeveloped, and he
had always had serious asthma as a result. He was little, but
mighty. Compact, but resolute. He had inherited the trademark
Clarke stubbornness: there had never been any making Bronson
do something if he didn't see fit to do it.

'Let's just stay,' I said, steeling my voice against my nerves.
I took off down the hill.

'Filthy blackies!' the boys yelled as I rode past them.

I felt a small rock hit me in the centre of my back, then another
clattered down against the chain of my bike. One of the boys
rode onto the track, swerving right up next to me, as if he was
about to crash his bike into mine, pulling away only at the last
minute. I looked back. Bronson had somehow fallen off his bike.
His knee was bleeding. His bottom lip trembled.

'C'mon,' I said, riding over and dismounting to help my
brother up. 'Let's go home.'

There was something about what had just happened that
made the hairs on my arms stand on end – something hideous
about the sudden escalation from words into physical bullying;
a scariness about the pack mentality. It was as if the group of
boys had somehow realised their power: they outnumbered us,
and were away from the gaze of grown-ups. It was like they'd

become intoxicated with the possibility of the havoc they could wreak. I looked around to find the McGuire kids, but they were nowhere to be seen. Bronson and I slowly wheeled our bikes out of the park and around the corner to our house, my brother limping and sniffling all the way.

Mum was on the phone when we arrived home, the cord curled nervously around an index finger as she stood in the hallway, peering out the front door for us. She put the receiver down and came over. 'That was Mrs McGuire. Jennifer and Nathan just got home. She's driving them over here.'

'They left,' I said to Mum. 'They rode off and left us at the park.'

Mum's eyes locked with mine. She looked upset, as if she could feel the hurt in my voice.

'It wasn't their fault . . .' she began.

'They *left us there*,' Bronson reiterated.

Mum opened her mouth, as if she was about to say something, then closed it, as if she'd thought better of it.

Mum and Mrs McGuire discussed the incident in hushed tones in the kitchen. Bronson, Jennifer, Nathan and I sat in silence on the edge of the front veranda, sucking lemonade icy poles. Occasionally, when I took my eyes off my icy pole and looked up at Jennifer, she smiled at me. I stared blankly back at her, slurping up the drips.

The McGuires were good people. They were our best friends. But they hadn't *said* anything. To those boys. When they were calling us names. I tried to calm down and smile back at my friend. I reminded myself about all the good things we did together – about what Jennifer had written on my Student of the Week album back in grade one; the crumpled piece of sunflower-yellow cardboard still sat at the bottom of one of the drawers in my wooden desk.

But the scene at the bike park just keep looping in my head. Her silence. The way they'd suddenly disappeared. I *knew* they were scared. I knew they were just kids. But so were we. My friend's silence hurt more than the names we'd been called – more than seeing my brother's bloody, grazed knee.

'We're sorry we didn't help you at the park,' I wanted my friend to say, with her head bowed low in acknowledgement of her failure.

I wondered what might have happened if the McGuires had said: 'Push off, you morons, these are our friends!' If they'd picked up rocks themselves and defended us.

Over the next few weeks, the initial disappointment subsided, but I never quite felt as close to my friend again. The abandonment was always there, between us.

There are myriad ways of singing it, but this is the melody I hum. That West Indian way, of crooning a tale. Or else what's the music for?

In grade five, spit balls became the weapon of choice for bullies. To fashion a spit ball, you ripped a thin strip of paper from an exercise book, put it in your mouth and sucked it until it went soggy. When the paper was sufficiently wet and malleable, it was removed from the mouth and rolled between thumb and forefinger into a sticky compact ball. The missile could then be launched at any unsuspecting culprit – preferably from behind. My own afro hair provided the perfect target: coarse, thick and curly so that the gluey globs of sucked paper stuck fast, and held hard when they dried. Tormentors were sometimes able to launch a barrage of the starchy missiles before I even noticed.

A short boy named Derek Healey, with closely cropped fair hair and a scraggly rat's tail that hung down between his shoulders, sat in the row behind me in class. Derek would launch spit ball after spit ball, class after class. They landed on my workbooks and desk, bounced off the back of my school tunic. The other kids would watch him lining the paper spheres up on his desk, but nobody alerted the teacher or told him to stop. I did my best to ignore Derek and his snickering friends, but one afternoon, the bullying escalated.

'Psst. Hey, blackie. Hey you, blackie. Over here, blackie!' Each missile was now accompanied by a whispered taunt. I was determined not to turn around, but the spit-ball barrage continued sporadically throughout afternoon lessons, his taunts becoming progressively louder.

My grade five teacher, Mrs Hird, was sitting at her desk marking a stack of spelling homework. I'd had her two years before, in grade three, and had been elated to be in her class again. She sighed heavily when she noticed me standing next to her desk; we were supposed to be quietly working away in our story-writing books.

'What is it, Maxine?' she asked impatiently, her red pen hovering in mid-air.

'Derek's been throwing spit balls at me.'

'Okay, I'll tell him to stop.'

'And he's been saying mean things.'

'What kind of things?' She sounded hesitant, as if she didn't really want to know.

'He's been calling me "blackie".'

My teacher paused, staring steadily at me for a moment. I shifted my weight from one foot to the other, aware that in the quiet classroom, our whispering could be heard by the whole roomful of students.

'Has he been calling you anything else?'

'No. Not this afternoon, anyway.'

Mrs Hird kept her grey-green eyes on me, red pen still poised above the spelling test she'd been marking. 'Well,' she said slowly, 'that's what you are. You can call him whitey if you like.' She smiled at me, as if we were sharing a private joke.

I stared back at her, indignant with shock. 'That's *racist*,' I declared loudly. I'd never used the word before. Earlier that month, my father and mother had been talking about a man who lived somewhere in a place called South Africa. Nelson Mandela was his name. He'd just been let out of prison. He'd been jailed in the first place for saying that black people should be able to have the same things as white people had. My mum told me that Nelson Mandela had been locked up for more than twenty years. There'd been photographs of him in the newspaper. Thousands and thousands of people had lined the streets to celebrate his release.

'Racist scum,' my dad had said under his breath, looking at pictures of Mandela shaking hands with the white prison guards after he got out of jail. He'd said it so quietly I almost didn't believe it had come from him.

'What's *racist*?'

Mum had shot Dad a warning look across the breakfast table.

'It's when people treat you differently because of your *race*. Because of where you come from,' Dad had explained, folding the newspaper up and setting it aside.

Maxine Beneba Clarke

Racist. The word felt strange in my mouth: powerful, as if now that I could name the thing that was happening to me, it had become real, not something I was imagining or being *oversensitive* about.

As soon as I said the word, the look on Mrs Hird's face changed. The contours around her eyes and mouth swirled angrily, like the sky before a storm.

'How *dare* you use that word in my classroom,' she said, so softly I wished she was yelling it. 'How *dare* you accuse a classmate of something like that. How could you—? Go away. Go back to your seat.'

I could feel the whole class staring as I returned to my desk in the second-last row.

'Blackie!' Derek hissed again, smirking as I eased myself back into my chair.

I sat at my desk, staring down at my exercise book. White noise rushed through my head. Mrs Hird was a favourite teacher of mine. I wasn't sure what to do. If I complained to the principal, I would not only be complaining about Derek, but also complaining about my teacher.

I didn't tell my parents what had happened. I knew that doing so would result in a whole lot of trouble I didn't want to face. I would have to sit in Mrs Hird's class for another three weeks, till the end of the school year, with her knowing I'd dobbed on her.

I continued on in class as I always did, participating in the classroom activities and even smiling at Mrs Hird when she complimented me on my excellent schoolwork. But the anger inside me burned. I hated her. I hated her with a ferocity that frightened me. My feelings about her were stronger than any dislike I'd had for any child who'd tormented me. I wanted to run up behind Mrs Hird and push her down the concrete stairs when we were heading out to play sport. I contemplated getting snail pellets from my dad's back shed and putting them in her coffee when she wasn't looking. I wanted to make her so sick she never came back into the classroom. I wanted to make her hurt. I wanted to humiliate her in front of the whole school. I wanted her to disappear.

I'd been told, by my parents and various other protectors over the years, that the children who were racist towards me were bullies who *didn't know any better.* I'd believed, on some level, that when they grew up, the kids who teased me would realise that brown was just a skin colour and they would stop being so ridiculous. Now, the evidence was mounting that this might not be so, and the prospect of living forever in a world like my schoolyard was unfathomable.

My behaviour had for years been impeccable. But the strain of the bullying started to wear thin. The anger and the pressure of being constantly needled would build. When the jeers started, I would find one of my tormentor's glaring insecurities – whatever was the easiest to latch on to in the moment of flash-rage: weight, glasses, freckles – and say something unforgivable back.

'At least I can read!' I'd scoff at Derek Healey. 'At least I didn't repeat *kindergarten.* Is there something wrong with your brain? *Dummy.* Are you *retarded* or something?' They were horrible words, I knew it. I could see them cutting into him. I could see the change in his demeanour when I retaliated. It made me feel both remorseful and powerful at the same time.

Sometimes, I'd wait patiently until a tormentor had started walking away and then I'd shove them in the back, out of nowhere, as hard as I could. I'd watch them sprawl across the pavement and calmly walk away, their tears leaving me feeling oddly satisfied.

Questioned in the principal's office, I'd stand there sullenly, refusing to answer, shrugging, staring blankly. I felt the principal's relief at my silence – at not having to deal with the root cause of the problem, not having to punish another child for the kind of racism that was as commonplace as cornflakes. The easiest solution – perhaps for all of us – was to peg me as a struggling black child with a serious behavioural problem, which everyone involved knew I was not.

I started to spend my lunchtimes against The Wall. The Wall was a stretch of brown brick that bordered the asphalt play area directly outside the principal's office window. When you had been in serious trouble, you were made to stand there at lunchtime: back to the brick, hands by your sides, watching as all the other kids played handball or skipping or chasings right in front of you. Standing against The Wall was a dramatic act of public shaming, but it was much less humiliating than remaining silent in the face of so many years of bullying; much less humiliating than letting myself be crushed down even more.

11.

THE SCHOOL LIBRARY was set apart from the brick buildings of the rest of the school. It was a rickety wooden one-room affair that had once upon a time been the original schoolhouse. To reach the library, you skirted around the main building and veered right into the feathered shade of two giant red gums. From there, the shouts and cheers of schoolyard games of handball and bull-rush were muted.

The library had a magic kind of quiet. In certain sections of the library – those where the R.L. Stine, Sweet Valley High and Baby-Sitters Club titles were shelved – the brown-speckled carpet was worn threadbare with traffic. In other places, the dead-straight spines of hardback reference books appeared unmoved from day to day, their edges gathering thin layers of dust. The library was a refuge for geeks, misfits and outcasts, a place where those for whom supervision meant survival could seek the reassuring nearness of a staff member.

I walked up the uneven wooden steps, pushed through the swinging glass door, and turned left towards the non-fiction section My red-and-white-checked tunic clung damply to my back. My white knee-high socks dug into my sweaty mahogany shins. *Australia's Most Dangerous Insects. How Things Work. The First Fleet. Understanding Outer Space.* I followed the non-fiction section deeper into the library, trailing an index finger along the hard, perfectly aligned spines. I stopped in the geography section, kneeled down to browse.

'Can I help you there, Maxine? What are you after?' The librarian, Miss Richie, was a slim woman with mousy brown hair. Her enormous reading glasses were encircled with large tortoise-shell frames. When Miss Richie wasn't looking through her glasses to read, she peered intently over them: brow lowered, eyebrows raised, in a way that made her seem like she was in a constant state of disapproval.

Miss Richie was softly spoken. She wore high-waisted camel-coloured slacks and billowy faux-silk blouses. Miss Richie was attractive-ordinary. Like if you took her to one of those make-over places in the shopping centre where they primped and permed you, draped you in a feather boa, then broke out the Vaseline lens, you wouldn't recognise the vixen the camera captured. You'd peer at the new glam Miss Richie, all boggle-eyed and wow-who-knewish.

'I'm doing a project. On Jamaica. For Mrs Dutton's grade six class. Do you have any books on Jamaica?'

The librarian flicked through the card catalogue. Paused. 'Actually, we do have one!' she said, not bothering to conceal her surprise. She walked over to the middle shelves. 'It looks new.' She checked the borrowing slip glued to the inside front cover. 'I don't think it's been borrowed before.'

The bold black word *Jamaica* was printed in capitals across the front cover.

'Thank you.' I took the book, and headed over to the beanbag area.

'There's also the encyclopaedias and the atlases for more information,' Miss Richie called after me, climbing back onto the long-legged pine stool behind the borrowing desk.

On the cover of the book, beneath the bold lettering, were illustrations: mangoes, coconuts, a smiling girl wearing a feathered carnival headdress. Inside, the book was divided into different subject headings: Climate; Food; Geography; People; History.

Jamaica is a beautiful place, the text began. According to the author, the weather in Jamaica was almost always like a mild kind of summer. Everything that grew there – mangoes, bananas, sugar cane – was rich and sweet. The fields were lush and green, the soil brown–black and fertile – quite unlike the pale sandy dirt and terracotta clay in our backyard at home.

The people in the book's illustrations looked laidback and carefree. Jamaicans celebrated life through music: the toombah, tabor, goombay and bongo drums. The cow-horn abeng trumpet. Reggae. Calypso. Dancehall. Many of the music styles were familiar from my father's record collection.

I sank lower into the grubby lime-green beanbag in the quiet reading area of the library. Infinity blue ocean. Jade green mountains. Brightly coloured fabrics. At the very back of the book, just before the index, was a page headed: *History of the people*. The page was black and white, not coloured like the rest of the book, and seemed like it had been stuck there as a footnote.

Jamaica was colonised by the British during the Atlantic slave trade, and populated by slaves from West Africa. The original inhabitants of Jamaica, known as the Arawak Indians, are no longer in existence. The current inhabitants of the island are primarily the descendants of slaves from Africa.

Next to the text was a sketch of the inside of a large boat, with crisscrossed black patterns inside it.

African slaves being transported inside the lower deck of a slave ship, the caption read. I peered at the page more closely. The crisscrossed black inside the ship's hull wasn't patterns. It was people, shackled together at the necks and feet. Black bodies were crammed in next to each other side by side, a seemingly impossible number of them.

It was as if the air had been sucked out of the library. I could hear the end-of-lunch bell ringing in the distance, the muted footsteps of a class of kids lining up outside on the balcony to come in for library time. The kids started filing in − a grade three class − chattering and jostling each other, red library bags swinging in their hands.

Miss Richie was standing over my beanbag. 'The bell's just gone, Maxine. Shouldn't you be in class? Let me just quickly check that book out for you and you can go.' She took the book from my hands, carried it over to the desk, stamped the card and made a note in the register.

'Thanks.' I hurried down the library steps, around the back of the main school building and across the asphalt play area. I walked slowly up the double staircase that led to the grade five and six classrooms. *Slaves*. The people in Jamaica were slaves. From *Africa*. People in my *family* had been slaves. Possibly. *Maybe*. I didn't know much about the slave trade: only that, for years, white people had treated black people badly − beaten them, chained them up and forced them to work for free. Occasionally I'd glimpse a few minutes of a movie while channel surfing, but in those movies slavery was always something that had happened in America. It had nothing to do with me. *Nothing.*

At home that afternoon, our family atlas confirmed what the library book had already told me about the climate and geography of the country. There were photographs of the impossibly lush Blue Mountains. Men stood in the centre of cane fields, the taut muscles of their upper arms shiny with sweat. I could smell the wetness of the earth, the salty sea-and-soil air. There was a picture of a kid, three or four years old maybe, chewing on a sugarcane stalk. I could taste the stringy roughage of it, feel the sweet liquid trickling down my throat.

> The population of Jamaica, like those inhabiting most of the West Indies, are the descendants of African slaves.

Maybe it *was* true then. Maybe *I* was the *descendant of African slaves.* How was it even possible? Me, sitting here on my grey-silver quilt in my rose-pink bedroom in suburban Sydney.

> Jamaica is an English-speaking country. Although it was first discovered by Christopher Columbus, and claimed by the Spanish, it was later colonised by the British. Various patois or creoles are spoken. These patois developed as a result of West African slaves mixing their native languages with English.

I thought of my grandparents, the lyrical poetic way they spoke English, their voices singing down the phone receiver at me as if each syllable was a pitch-perfect note, carefully selected from a scale they alone were attuned to. Surely such beautiful language could not be the result of such a horrible history. My grandparents had never spoken of this. They would surely have told us all.

Slavery felt like a shameful thing to be descended from. As if it somehow made me less of a person. These people, chained, beaten, stolen, made to work for no money. These people, who had their babies sold away from them. These people, worked to death in the fields like I saw in American movies. I was them. I was *these people*, and they were me. I felt like I'd discovered an awful secret, something I should never speak of. I wondered if all of the people who called me and my family names and treated us badly did it because they *knew*. Because they knew we weren't *actual* people, knew what we had once been.

Whenever anyone asked me where I was from, I'd explain that I was born in Australia; that my parents were born in the West Indies and had grown up in London and moved to Australia after they were married.

'You look African,' they'd often say, confused.

I'd shake my head as though that was the most ridiculous proposition in the world.

———————

After dinner, I helped clear away the dishes and wiped down the long table in our dining room. Then I dried the table with a tea towel, unrolled my project cardboard and weighted the corners with four mugs. I took my HB pencil and measured a line of dots, exactly one centimetre apart, down the centre of the cardboard and down each side, then joined each row of dots up with a ruler to form horizontal writing lines.

I carefully outlined the word *Jamaica* across the top of the page in bright green bubble writing, and drew coconut palms on either side. I drew a border of dancing girls, kicking their legs up under brightly coloured skirts, the way they looked in the library book's illustration. I wrote about saltfish, banana fritters, ackee, and rice and peas. I wrote about the humidity of the tropical climate, carnival time in the West Indies. I wrote about growing sugar cane and bananas. I made sure that my letters just nicked the top and the bottom of the lead pencil lines, the way Mrs Dutton liked them to.

I tried not to think about the black bodies chained in the hull of the ship, or about the Arawaks, who simply *did not exist anymore* — as if they'd one day just all held hands and walked across the sands of Jamaica into the breathtaking turquoise of the Caribbean Sea.

Each evening, for a week or so, I eased down the elastic band restraining the cardboard roll and continued working. One Friday evening, I stood before my finished project. Surveying my work, from the green bubble writing to the jumping orange flying-fish and turquoise water, I felt well pleased with my efforts. The writing was neat. The pictures had been traced clearly. All of the shading was between the lines. My grade six teacher was well known never to give full marks for any project. 'We all need something to strive for,' she'd explain. 'Nobody's work is perfect.' My previous school project marks had ranged between eighty-six and ninety-nine per cent, but looking over my Jamaica project, I was convinced this would be the one that finally proved there was an exception to the rule.

Mum walked up behind me, drying her hands on a tea towel. I could sense her reading my project over my shoulder.

'That looks great!' she enthused. 'Well done. There's a bit of space down the bottom there, though.' She pointed to a four-centimetre gap running across the bottom of the square of cardboard. 'You can probably fit some more information there if you want to. Have a look back and see if there's anything you might have missed out.'

I glanced up at her.

Jamaica was colonised by the British during the Atlantic slave trade, and populated by slaves from West Africa.

'You . . .' She hesitated. 'You haven't written much about the actual, um, *cultural make-up* of the Jamaican people.'

'I wrote about the instruments and drums and carnival time.' I pointed towards the relevant paragraph, titled: *Bacchanal*. 'That's cultural.'

'Well, okay. It does look great.'

I picked up my lead pencil. At the end of the handwritten information, in the gap left at the bottom of the page, I carefully wrote the words THE END, in fat bubble writing, outlining the letters in heavy black biro then carefully shading them in with a purple pencil.

When my teacher handed back my Jamaica assignment several weeks later she smiled at me: that kind of smile you give little kids you think are super cute.

'I *never* give one hundred per cent for assignments,' she said in a gentle voice. 'Because no child ever does an assignment perfectly.'

I slid the elastic band from the cardboard, unrolled it and looked down at my mark. In a red circle in the top right-hand corner of the project, Mrs Dutton had written *99.99%*, followed by a big exclamation mark. I looked back up at my teacher.

'Jamaica sounds like such a *beautiful* place to visit,' she said with a smile, as she continued handing back the class projects. 'While I was reading your project, Maxine, I found myself desperately wanting to go there for a holiday! You know –' my teacher looked at me pointedly '– for a while, I lived in *Fiji*.'

I stared at her; she seemed to be waiting for me to say something. I cleared my throat. 'That must've been . . . *nice*,' I said, slowly.

'You know, we still haven't chosen an item for our class to perform at the end-of-year concert. I have two songs in mind that I think you'll *love*, Maxine.'

After lunch, our teacher played the songs for us on one of the school's rectangular metal cassette players, as we sat cross-legged on the dark orange carpet at the front of the classroom. One of the songs, about *harmony* and *getting along with people*, had been written by a group of primary school children just like us. The second song was called 'Jamaica Farewell'.

'This song was made very famous by a Jamaican singer named Harry Belafonte,' Mrs Dutton told us as she pressed the play button. Calypso guitar strains filled the room. I recognised the song. My father had it in his record collection.

'*Down the way, where the nights are gay . . .*'

The boys sitting at the back started tittering.

'*And the sun shines daily on the mountain top. I took a trip on a sailing ship, and when I reached Jamaica, I made a stop.*'

The song slowly faded out.

'So, those will be our two items for the end-of-year concert,' our teacher said. 'I was thinking we could have some of the girls dancing onstage while we sing "Jamaica Farewell". I'll have a think, and pick two or three suitable people.'

I straightened up hopefully, sitting taller among my classmates to try to encourage her eyes to fall on me. *This* was my kind of caper. I *loved* being onstage. I'd sung in the school choir throughout primary school, and we often had to coordinate actions with our singing. Mrs Dutton *knew* I'd be able to do it.

Besides, the song was about Jamaica, and she'd chosen it because of my project. Plus, I *looked* Jamaican. I was a shoo-in.

The school concert items ran in order of student age from grade three to grade six. Our class was scheduled last. We filed on for the first song, three rows of us, about eight kids per row. I lowered my head and crept into the back row. Mrs Dutton looked us over, standing at the front of the stage, with her back to the audience. Her enormous red-and-gold Christmas bell earrings jangled as she turned her head. She frowned, then pointed at Mahana, myself and Billy Leung. 'You three! Over here. Come into the front row!' She beckoned us towards the front of the stage, gently pushing a handful of other kids into the row behind. She looked the class over again, her smile widening.

The introduction music started. Mrs Dutton stepped off to the side of the stage and raised her arms to conduct us.

'*Oh, Australia, let's build our community, higher and low. Let's help each other, and learn each other's language so we can get along.*' I opened my mouth wide and sang loudly.

Mrs Dutton looked across at me, beaming encouragingly. I felt a hand push me in the back. I stepped forward a little, momentarily winded.

'*Our country's made from all nationalities . . .*'

Something hit me in the back of the neck. I could tell by its weight and wetness that it was probably a spit ball.

'*Many people from around the world . . .*'

Several of the kids behind me giggled.

'*Let's share and care for their personalities . . .*'

Another missile landed on my left shoulder. One of the boys must have prepared a pocketful.

'*Help them settle in . . .*'

When the first song had finished, Cindy and Sara stepped out from the back row in their Jamaican dancing girl costumes: fuchsia skirts with ostentatious ruffles down the showy side-split; matching feather-strewn bikini tops; a large hibiscus flower tucked behind each of their right ears. Their matching waist-length blonde hair had been brushed shiny and set into bouncy curls. Mahana, Billy Leung and I stepped back a little, to give them room to perform. 'Jamaica Farewell' started. As we sang, Cindy and Sara sashayed, wiggled their hips and kicked up their fake-tanned legs in the choreographed routine they'd been rehearsing with their teacher at Debbie's Dynamic Dance Academy for several weeks.

I looked out into the audience, squinting against the harsh stage lights of the auditorium. I could see my parents, sitting in the middle of the third row. Mum was fighting back a smirk. A stony, withering look was cemented on my father's face.

As the song progressed, the boys behind me ramped up their accents, until they were singing in caricatured patois, mimicking Belafonte.

'Down deeey wee where deey nightz dem geeeey, and de sun shine deeeely on de mowntayn top . . .'

Mrs Dutton beamed, thrashing her arms about, enthusiastically coaxing us to sing louder and more spiritedly, urging us towards the finishing crescendo.

As we filed off the concert stage, I tried to immediately push the performance from my mind. Lewis Stevens was walking down the stage stairs in front of me. I stared at the back of his head. Lewis Stevens was my not-so-secret grade six crush. He'd been my crush every grade since the Catch and Kiss episode back in grade two, though things had been slightly awkward in the couple of years following. I'd always sat right at the top of the class academically. Yet each year, the academic award for the highest achiever in my class would go to some other kid – and most years it had been Lewis who took first prize. This had turned our classroom relationship into one of intense rivalry. After every spelling, maths or geography test, one of us would find an excuse to wander over to the other side of the classroom and find out the other's mark.

'What did you get?'

'You tell me your mark first.'

'I got twenty-four out of twenty-five.' I'd lift my hand from my exercise book to reveal the circled red mark written at the bottom of the long list of words.

'Me too.' He'd reveal his own mark, bitterly disappointed. 'I can't believe you got *especially* wrong,' he'd tease, looking over my spelling test.

'Well, *seriously*, who can't spell *mischievous*?'

'Lewis! Maxine!' The teacher would call, ordering us back to our separate corners.

Lewis was a sporty kid – he played on the local soccer team and always placed first or second in the school athletics events. Yet his academic achievements frequently relegated him to the dork corner – more so as we moved through the grades towards high school. He was a nice kid, Lewis, the eldest of four children, good-natured and polite. We had a genuine affection for each other, though we sheepishly hid it as much as we could.

In grade six, when the friendship cliques started to develop, Lewis started going out with one of the other girls in our class: a blue-eyed lean-legged girl with a passion for dance eisteddfods and a very rehearsed way of flicking her always-untied golden hair back from her face. At lunchtime, Lewis and Sara would go down to the back of the school with the other grade six 'couples'. The group would station themselves in the out-of-bounds area between the long jump pits and the back fence to pash and feel each other up. A discreet audience of other grade sixers would casually walk past to spy on the pashing sessions.

'I saw Lewis pash Sara behind the long jump pit. With his tongue and everything. They didn't come up for breath for *three whole minutes.*'

When we filed back into the classroom after lunch on the days he'd spent time down the back, Lewis would refuse to look at me, bending his head intently over his work. I'd stare at him out of the corner of my eye, while also feigning complete absorption in writing the states on a map of Australia or performing some similarly mundane task.

Whenever we were in close proximity, though, seated cross-legged next to each other in the hall during weekly assembly, or standing next to each other in the canteen line at lunchtime, we would play our *second best* game.

'You're my *second-favourite* girl in the school,' Lewis would declare, a grin spreading across his slightly freckled face.

'*Yuck.* You're my *second-least* favourite boy in the school.' I'd screw up my face in disgust.

'Second-favourite.'

'Second-least.'

'Second-favourite.'

'Second-least.'

The game would continue with each of us getting progressively louder, and speaking more quickly until I would accidentally-on-purpose mess up and reply with his line instead.

'Second-favourite.'

'You *like* me,' he would crow, laughing knowingly.

'Yuck. I do not. Piss off.' At that point, I would turn and walk away, secretly savouring the exchange.

I never begrudged Lewis his times pashing down the back. It brought him the kind of playground kudos he'd never otherwise have: the kind of respect I craved, but knew would never be mine.

———————

Lewis Stevens continued to occupy my thoughts as our class filed back into the audience after performing 'Jamaica Farewell'. Lewis would be going to a different high school from me; while I would be attending the local high school, he'd be enrolled at a private Anglican school.

After the concert had finished, the principal would be announcing the academic awards. Lewis would be wearing that smug smirk when he realised he'd topped the class again, but tonight I didn't care – I would get to watch him cross the stage in his tiptoed bounce just this one last time.

Sure enough, his name was called, and there he was: walking up to the stage, beaming, as cameras flashed from the section of the auditorium where his extended family was sitting. Lewis collected his award and headed back into the audience.

'And now the final award for the evening,' said the school principal. 'The award is for dux of the school – that is, the grade six student who has achieved the highest overall academic mark.'

I stared at the principal, willing him to shut up. He and I had had so many run-ins this term that I now viewed him as something of an arch nemesis. *I can't wait to get out of here.* Remarkably, it was the first time the thought had hit me. I was *leaving* this place. I had no idea what high school was going to be like, but at least I would be leaving the vast majority of my current tormentors behind. I was out of here. I stared up at Mr Parkinson. His lips were moving, but my mind was too busy turning over my realisation to digest what he was saying.

'Maxine!' Selina, the girl sitting next to me, was poking me in the side. 'It's you!'

I blinked at her, then turned back to face the stage. Mr Parkinson was staring at me expectantly.

'Maxine Clarke?' he called again.

Everyone – the whole audience – was staring at me.

'Go on,' whispered someone in the row behind me. 'Go and collect your award.'

The last time I'd checked, I'd trailed Lewis by two marks. But that was before I handed in the Jamaica project. The Jamaica project. *The Jamaica project had made me dux of the entire school.*

'Shit!' I said loudly. The kids on either side of me giggled. I stood up and made my way to the stage, still in shock.

The principal handed me a wooden plaque with an engraved copper nameplate attached and a brand-new hardcover book. I stared out at the audience, who applauded politely, if not overly enthusiastically. I hurried back down the stairs and resumed my seat.

The principal gave a short closing speech and then the formalities were over. The hall erupted into chaos: kids running around trying to find their parents, toddler siblings who'd been constrained on laps all evening finally seizing their chance to run free. I made my way over to where my parents were standing with my brother and sister.

'Congratulations!' An odd mixture of pride and shock was still written on their faces.

The father of one of my classmates passed by, herding his family towards one of the exits. 'That was a stroke of *luck*, wasn't it?' he scoffed, as they squeezed by us and disappeared into the night.

My mother adjusted her handbag on her shoulder and muttered under her breath, 'Luck had *nothing* to do with it.'

A handful of school friends and families made their way over to offer their genuine congratulations, but the reaction of a number of the parents and students that evening was in many ways a sign of what was to come. My friend's father's comment had a clear implication: it was impossible that I could have been named dux of the school on merit. The only conceivable explanation was that it was political correctness gone mad. To him, the alternative was just not feasible – was *unthinkable*.

But we weren't in Student of the Week territory now. I wasn't going to tuck my bottom in. I was here, despite everything. I was valedictorian: plain old black-faced me.

———————

I lay in bed on the evening of the concert, digesting what had happened, clutching the beautiful hardback book prize to my chest. I still couldn't fully process the events of the night. I'd come so close to winning the academic award in each of my classes for seven years – sometimes even weighing in at just half a mark away. And now . . .

I lifted the book up to examine it: *The Family Book of Mary Claire* by Eleanor Spence. I was a voracious reader, and glad to have something to keep me going for the first week of the summer holidays. The book jacket was illustrated with a landscape in which a red-dirt road wound off into the distance. In the foreground, a young girl wheeled a barrow against a backdrop of gum trees. A shiny bronze Children's Book Council of Australia Short-Listed Book sticker hovered in the upper left-hand corner, just beneath the title. Pasted inside the front cover was a red cardboard plate embossed with our school's kookaburra emblem. *Awarded to Maxine Clarke, Dux of the School 1991*, the inscription read.

The window next to my bed was half open. A warm breeze was blowing in. I opened the cover and started reading. The book told the story of several generations of an Anglo-Australian family, spanning the 1820s to the early 1900s. The older generation were convict escapees. They lived apart from settlers, fearing re-incarceration by the authorities, communicating only with the Aborigines who lived in the area where they'd built their house.

I read on through the evening by the light of my bedside lamp: past wood-rot and eucalypts and campfires; beyond charred kangaroo meat, and fish-filled rivers; through first contact, into convict shackles, around tired frontier struggles. As I read on, I became more and more uncomfortable. The Aboriginal characters in the book I'd been given were cheerful and simple-minded. Sarah, the matriarch of the Cleveland family, treated her son's Indigenous wife with contempt, declaring the marriage was *not real* and referring to her grandchildren as *blackamoor half-breeds*. That tight-chested feeling started to creep in. The walls of my bedroom felt like they were slowly caving in on me. I felt the anger, throbbing again.

I slammed the cover of my award book shut, raised my arm and hurled the prize across my bedroom. The book spun frisbee-like towards my bedroom wall, the jacket flapping as it glided through the air.

There are myriad ways of telling it. The plucky young black girl: the daughter of an actress and a mathematician who became the valedictorian. The small rural village and the young black arrivals. Florence Griffith Joyner, the fastest woman on earth, and a schoolyard game of Catch and Kiss. A visit to the dermatologist's office. A brand-new Cabbage Patch Kid. A tubby, panting little brown girl, sashaying across a mirrored studio in a mesh-panelled electric blue leotard.

That folklore way West Indians always have of weaving a tale. This is how it happened – or else what's a story for.

Part Two

12.

THE SUMMER OF the year you turn thirteen is always the most magical of times. All the toys are packed away or handed down or abandoned. Life is full of possibility. There is power growing in your fingertips, and swagger in your bearing. You hover in the wavering not-quite place between childhood and adolescence. You bask and keen in it. In that sudden slimming out. In the startling altering of seasons. In the unexpected long-leggedness. At thirteen, there is an alarming *seeing* of things. A coming-into-your-own. A *knowing-it*. A consciousness of being.

In the forever-gap between the end of grade six and the start of high school, I spent my mornings rollerskating round the smooth, deserted streets of Kellyville: wheezing heavily up the hills; grinding down my rubber stoppers on the freefall. Up Womboyne Avenue. Down Malonga. Onto Wrights Road. Inside my head, no matter how hard I tried to beat it back, I would still hear that primary school choir song, the one I used to warble on my candy-red two-wheeler: 'Don't Fence Me In'.

Afternoons were for sprawling on the floor next to my sunflower-yellow boom box playing my small library of cassette tapes over and over: Bobby Brown, Roxette, Girlfriend, Salt-N-Pepa, Bananarama and a foursome of soulful brown ex-choir boys who'd gone Motown and formed the heart-stealing R&B group Boyz II Men.

In the paradise evenings, when the sun melted orange and friendly over our clean, quiet suburb, I'd be stretched out barefoot on the camel-coloured couch in our lounge room, watching *The Fresh Prince of Bel-Air, The Cosby Show, Family Matters.* Black television families that seemed a little like mine.

Within a few weeks of leaving primary school, the never-going-back knowledge started to soften my memories. My red-and-white-checked school tunic hung inside the built-in wardrobe in my new bedroom that had once been Dad's study. It was the dress I'd worn to school on the very last day. In accordance with tradition, I'd shoved a black permanent marker into my schoolbag so other kids in the class could write farewell messages on the uniform. I'd been apprehensive about the idea, still haunted by the long list of 'compliments' on my grade one Student of the Week album.

In the third week of the holidays, I opened my wardrobe and pulled the school tunic off its wire hanger. I spread the dress across my bed, and surveyed the farewell comments again.

Good luck next year at high school.

I will miss you, Maxine.

You are so smart – you will go far.

Hooray, we got out of here alive!

Will always remember these primary school days.

Farewell, and good luck.

You are my second-favourite, forever.

It was as if all the bullying, all the name-calling, the exclusion and humiliation, had been nothing to them. It *had* been nothing to them: fleeting inconsequential commentary, temporary sport. On that last day of school, my classmates had approached one by one to write things onto my dress. I'd felt the gentle scrawl of the thick marker push against my skin through the worn, thin cotton.

There were those who'd declined the opportunity to leave a message. Carlita Allen. Derek Healey. A handful of others. The handwriting on my dress had been much more widely spaced than the lengthy farewell messages on most of the other kids' uniforms, but all the same, the notes left had been either neutral or positive.

Nostalgia and sentimentality had swept the classroom that last week. There'd been an avalanche of tears. My new friend Selina and I had sidestepped the overflow of pre-adolescent emotion and looked on with a mixture of bemusement and confusion as hugs were exchanged and pinkie promises to keep in touch were made.

That last afternoon, when I pulled the school tunic off over my head at home, there'd been black marks all over my back, stomach and upper arms where the permanent Texta had soaked through the material and into my skin. The black ink splotches looked like tiny little bruises, hidden away in places only I could see.

Now, staring at the threadbare dress on my bed, it looked so small. It had been less than a month since I'd last worn it, but it seemed like an archaic artefact: otherworldly. I scrunched the dress up into a ball and aimed it at the wire wastepaper basket in the corner of my room, then changed my mind and smoothed it out again. I re-hung it in my wardrobe and slid the door closed.

I sat down on my bed. Perhaps it hadn't been that bad. Perhaps I *had* been oversensitive. Perhaps I'd *expected* too much. Maybe if

I'd been tougher – more resilient – behaved differently. I would *have* to behave differently at high school, if the teasing started again. *Teasing.* That was all it had been. Just a bit of teasing. It didn't seem so serious now, in hindsight. I would be tougher next time. I would ignore it. I was older, and I wouldn't let it *get to me* the way it had before.

This is how it changes us. This is how we're altered.

One holiday afternoon, I took the last of my pocket money, pulled my sandals on, grabbed my white plastic Walkman from my bedroom and pulled the headphones onto my head.

'I'm just walking up to the petrol station for a slurpee!' I yelled over my shoulder into the lounge, where Mum was vacuuming.

'Fifty minutes if you're going on your own!' Mum yelled back. 'After that I'm going to drive around and come looking for you.'

Savouring the bittersweet only-just-thirteen trickle of freedom, I walked down the driveway, around the corner, up past the bike track, down the street leading to the car park at the back of the local shops and up the wide alleyway, with Bell Biv DeVoe bass-beating loudly in my ears.

Inside the petrol station shop, I removed the headphones and helped myself to a paper cup, put it underneath the Coke-flavoured lever and half filled the cup with icy brown sludge. I moved the cup underneath the blue lemonade lever, pushed it down and carefully moved the cup around in a circular motion to make sure a mountain of flavoured ice was piled high on top.

'What flavour are you getting?' a girl's voice behind me asked.

'Lemonade, probably,' came her friend's reply.

I froze. The second voice was unmistakable. I wrapped my hand around the slurpee cup and turned. *Carlita Allen.*

'Hi, Maxine!' she said. 'I thought it was you.'

Carlita looked different. Older. More sophisticated. Her long hair had been trimmed into a short, sleek bob that tapered in at the neck. She smiled at me, as if she was happy we'd bumped into each other.

'This is my friend Maxine,' she turned to tell the tall girl next to her. 'We were in grade six together,' she said, with an inexplicably proud look on her face. 'Maxine, this is Melanie. We're going to the same high school. We met on Orientation Day. We're the *only* people from Kellyville going there.' Carlita laughed nervously.

Carlita's mother was sending her to an all-girls school in Parramatta – one of those super-fancy private schools where you could stay on the campus during the week. Carlita was going to be a boarder. She'd boasted about it for the whole last term of school.

'Neither of us knows anyone else, so we're, like, *kindred spirits*. It's going to be, like, *so* full on!' Carlita giggled strangely again, smiling at her new friend.

I looked at Melanie: at the straight black hair falling down around her slim shoulders, at her beautiful almond-shaped eyes and walnut-toned skin. 'Hell-ooo!' she said, in an accent I couldn't quite place.

I stared hard at Carlita. Carlita stared back at me, waiting.

'That's nice.' I wrapped my lips around the red slurpee straw and kept glaring at her while I sucked up a freezing mouthful of the treat. 'I *really* hope that works out for you, Carlita.'

Carlita closed her eyes for a split second, like she was kicking herself for opening her big mouth. I walked over and handed the bemused shop attendant my dollar coin, and left the service station.

Looking back over my shoulder, I could see Carlita's friend Melanie staring after me through the glass doors.

———————————

'We're, like, *kindred spirits!*' I re-enacted the scene dramatically to my friend Selina a few days later, flouncing around the wooden floorboards of her bedroom, turning my nose up towards the ceiling, and putting on a lazy valley girl accent. 'It's going to be, like, *so* full on!' I blew my imaginary fringe out of my eyes like Carlita had blown the fringe of her new hairdo.

Selina, who was lying on her bed, giggled. The purple wall behind her was pinned with posters of Prince, Fred Savage from *The Wonder Years* and Luke Perry from *Beverly Hills 90210*: joint crushes of ours.

Selina had arrived at my primary school towards the middle of grade six. Before she'd arrived at my school, she'd gone to a Steiner school, where they only did lessons if they felt like it and did the work for all of their subjects in coloured pencil in one enormous hardback art book.

Selina's parents were performers. They stilt-walked in city carnivals and went in parades dressed up as different storybook characters. They made all their own costumes in the small lounge room of their house, and they got paid to do it. I would go to my friend's house for a visit, and see the delicate skeletal wire under-structure of butterfly wings sitting in the middle of the hallway, or I'd pass a desk strewn with sheets of soft leather, various mask-shapes traced across them ready for cutting. The whole set-up seemed so weirdly wonderful to me.

There was some tenuous link between our families: some friends of Selina's parents were also friends of my parents. In just a few months, we'd become inseparable. Selina was one of only a handful of people from primary school who would be attending the same high school as me, and by the end of our summer together, I was super glad of it.

Over the summer holidays, Selina and I trekked into Darling Harbour with her parents and little sister. We lolled around eating treats or explored the harbour as her mum and dad roamed high above the holidaying crowds on their stilts, limber and graceful, waving their silver wings, smiles dancing across their glitter-masked faces.

This is how it happened. Or else what's a story for.

13.

THERE ARE MYRIAD ways of telling it. That West Indian way of unfolding a tale. This is how it sang.

On the first day of high school, Selina's parents insisted on driving us. Our uniforms were freshly ironed and extremely new-looking. Our dark blue tartan skirts had that fresh-out-of-the-shop sheen, and fell down below our knees. I'd made my mum cornrow my hair into six straight braids in anticipation of the first week. The ends of my plaits were collected at the base of my neck with a dark blue ribbon. Selina was wearing a hair scrunchie her mum had made out of the same material as our school skirts; her thick dark brown hair was swept into a long side ponytail.

My body tensed as the car slowly approached the cluster of tan school buildings. I could feel my friend's apprehension, too, as she stared out the window.

'It's okay, Mum. You can just drop us here. Thanks!'

We entered the school grounds and edged slowly forward into the open concrete corridor. A group of grade ten or eleven students sitting at a wooden table stopped their loud chatter, and looked over at us. Silence fell over the group as we passed. When we rounded the corner out of their sight, we heard an explosion of laughter behind us.

'Oh my god.'

'Did you see that side ponytail?'

'And their skirts. What are they, *Amish* or something?'

'I swear, the year sevens get daggier every year.'

The laughter continued. We exchanged worried glances. The bell sounded. We made plans to meet up before our first class, and parted ways to attend homeroom. Every day began with homeroom, which served as a multi-grade rollcall of sorts. Students were divided alphabetically across year levels, with siblings being in the same room.

By the time I matched the classroom on my timetable with the number on the classroom door, almost all the seats in the room were taken. I could see my sister, sitting with a friend, in the centre of the room. There were no seats near them, so I took a deep breath and walked towards the front row of the classroom where there were still seats available.

'Who's that?'

'Is that Cecelia's sister?'

'They look exactly the same. You can't even tell them apart!'

'Yeah, like with monkeys.'

If you searched hard enough, there was a vague family resemblance between Cecelia and me, but you'd have had to stand us side by side and, even then, you'd be scratching around for similarities.

I sat down in one of the seats in the front row, and turned ever so slightly towards my sister. Cecelia could feel me looking at her, I knew it. Her demeanour stiffened, though she kept talking to her friend as if she hadn't noticed a thing. Then she swivelled her eyes – but not her body – in my direction, and stared at me hard. It was a *don't-say-a-word* look. A *turn-back-around-and-let's-just-get-through-this* look, at once empathetic and reprimanding. I understood. These are the cues we learn to read: the subtle gaps and shrugs and glances. The bullied know body language like bulls know red flags. To the bullied, reading body language is like having a compass: it keeps us from stumbling through dark forests, falling down cliff drops, slipping beneath fatal rapids.

Before I turned back around in my chair, I glanced discreetly over to where the comments had come from. A group of older boys were lounging around in a back corner of the classroom. Instead of sitting on the plastic chairs they were stretched out on top of the desks, and sprawled on the floor. They seemed enormous, these boys. Man-sized. Hairy legs poked out of their dark blue Stubbies shorts. Their Adam's apples bobbed up and down as they talked and joked. One of them was hoeing into a Vegemite sandwich, another was drinking a carton of chocolate milk.

'What are you staring at, monkey girl?'

Every part of my body went cold. A shivery feeling crept from the top of my spine and slowly spread through my torso, prickling the length of my arms and legs. These boys were bigger than me. Older, and *much bigger*. The tone the boy used hadn't sounded like when Derek Healey used to tease me, like it was some kind of gleeful sport. The boy's voice was deep, and growly, and husky, and terrifying. There was a force behind his words. As if they were driven by more than just the desire to provoke a reaction from me. There was conviction behind his comment; palpable spite. I bit down on my lip and turned back towards the front of the room. I was relieved when the homeroom teacher finally arrived and the group of senior school boys reluctantly shuffled into their seats.

To ease the grade sevens into transition, grade eleven students had been trained as peer support leaders. At the end of our first week at high school, Selina and I, with a handful of other grade sevens, walked slowly around the school grounds, following our designated leaders.

The leaders – year eleven girls – were tallish, with their slim bodies pushing out into hourglass hips, and their busts Wonderbra-ed into C cups. Samantha was a brunette, and Amy and Amanda had blonde hair. Apart from that, they were almost identical in both manner and appearance.

'This is the school oval. The grade eleven and twelve boys play on that basketball court at lunch. It's kind of unofficially out of bounds to everybody else.' One of them waved a hand nonchalantly towards the concrete courts. '*We* sit on the court, but that's because our *boyfriends* play.'

As they turned to herd us in another direction I looked over at Selina, rolled my eyes and scrunched my lips into a kiss. She stifled a laugh.

'This is the library. It's open at lunchtime, but only the chinks and the integration kids hang out here at lunch.' Amy wrinkled her nose, tucked her hair behind her ears.

'What's *integration*?' one of the other grade seven kids asked.

'The kids with disabilities. You know, the spastics.'

'Amy!'

'What?' Amy turned towards Samantha, one hand balanced on her hip, where the top of her very short school skirt met her collared shirt. Her shirt was white, but she was wearing a lacy black bra underneath it. 'Some of them *are* spastic anyway!'

The other two girls looked at Amy warningly. Amy shrugged. 'It's true! We're supposed to be helping them settle in. They need to know that only the spastics and the chinks hang out in the library at lunchtime.' She laughed, and leaned against the wide wooden shelving in the concrete nook just outside the library door.

'Everyone calls this area where we're standing Chinatown. The chinks all stand here and eat their lunch before they go into the library.'

All three girls started to giggle. Bhagita Singh, an Indian Australian girl in our peer support group, pulled nervously at her long ponytail and looked over at me. Our eyes met briefly. We quickly averted our gazes.

'It's true,' Samantha said matter-of-factly. 'The integration kids can't go out on the grass, 'cause some of them are in wheelchairs, and the others are just Asian.'

'Yeah. Asians like to study a lot. That's all they do. It's cultural,' Amy explained. 'No offence or anything, but it's true.' She looked pointedly at Bhagita.

I stared through the glass doors of the library. It was split-level. On the upper level was a cluster of glass-walled meeting rooms with desks and chairs in them. On the lower level was a small group of study desks. Every conceivable other space from floor to ceiling was jammed with reading material. I wanted to be in there now, with my head buried in the musty pages of some well-thumbed book or other. I thought about all the amazing books I'd read over summer, lying on the floor of my bedroom, or Selina's. *People Might Hear You*. *Iggie's House*. Books that had taken me away from my life; words that had blocked out people like Amy and Amanda and Samantha.

As the group moved away from the library, up towards the maths block, I stared back at the library longingly. Chinatown seemed like my kind of place.

———————

The first term of high school fast became a blur of familiarity. Wooden desks carved with wonky initials. Sports change rooms which smelled of bleach and sweat. Ancient overhead projectors casting flickering squares of light at the front of the room, projecting the teachers' lesson notes which were handwritten onto clear sheets of plastic with permanent marker. Rusty Bunsen burners. Snap-frozen rats dissected in the science lab. A roaring canteen trade in chocolate Billabongs, pink-iced doughnuts and hot meat pies. The bright blue sports-day bike shorts which displayed the frequent nicks and cuts on the just-learned-to-shave legs of the mass of thirteen-year-old girls. Backpacks hanging heavy with thick maths textbooks. Standard-issue calculators in their hard black plastic cases. Pencil cases hiding sharp Kmart compasses, which were used to scratch bitchy comments about students and staff into desks, chairs and toilet walls.

14.

MR SPENCER, OUR grade seven sports teacher, was an enormous man: well over six and a half foot, with a broad chest and thick tree-trunk thighs. Rumour had it Spencer had been a rugby player, but injury had brought his promising sporting career to an end. Now he was stuck begrudgingly teaching us.

'Alright! Let's do this quickly!' Spencer boomed as we scurried into our respective change rooms to get dressed.

Cold reflected off the burgundy floor and wall tiles in the girls change room, despite the thirty-degree day outside. The dark colour scheme made the place seem spooky and unpoliced. Playground gossip was that there was some perve who had cameras hidden in there, and us girls would often joke about it while we were getting changed.

'Why are you standing there with your top off? Yuck! That shot is totally gonna be in the video highlight reel!'

On that first sports day, though, news of this alleged electronic surveillance hadn't yet reached us. The girls who already wore bras stripped off in the open, pulling their sky blue shirts over their heads with studied nonchalance, taking slightly longer than they needed to scrabble around in their sports bags for their bike shorts and V-neck sports shirts. The other girls, like myself, casually headed for the stalls.

'Come on, girls!' Mr Spencer boomed, standing at the door of the change room. 'The boys are already out here!'

We snuck worried glances at each other as we shoved our uniforms into our bags, pulled on our sneakers and quickly filed outside.

Mr Spencer looked us up and down: the line of skinny-legged boys and slightly taller, terrified-looking girls. He shook his head in dismay, as if he didn't like his chances of finding a solid sportsperson among us.

'Right. Let's see what you're all made of then. Follow me.' He walked us along the covered walkways linking each faculty block to the next, past the administration block and across the road to the public oval. He gestured for us to line up behind the white starter's line.

'Three laps. Each time you pass me, I'll give you a stamp.' He pressed a button on the top of his large, rectangular watch. 'Go!'

We started jogging, a tight-knit group at first, but as we rounded the first bend about a quarter of the group, mostly boys, began to pull away. I worked my legs hard, pumping them steadily, trying to focus on my breathing.

In primary school, I'd always come last, or second-last, in cross country. I'd start out sprinting as hard as I could, and stick in the front group for a while, but then I'd get winded, suffer a debilitating stitch, slow to a jog, then to a walk. Despite my initial enthusiasm, I'd inevitably finish with the kids who'd walked the entire course. 'How did you do, Maxine?' Cecelia would wander over to me at carnival lunch-break, a bright blue first-place ribbon pinned to the front of her uniform.

'I couldn't be bothered. I just walked.' I'd pretend not to care.

Cecelia had always been the sporty one – she had continued with Little Athletics, each year breezing through local, then regional, then state championships, often going on to compete at a national level. The wooden bookcase in her room was hung with shiny silver sports team trophies, and gold athletics medals threaded onto red velvet ribbons.

Cecelia and Dad ran together. They'd set off side by side through the back streets of Kellyville, their long brown legs striding out in unison. Cecelia would be in her black bike pants, singlet and sun visor. Dad would wear his daggy blue polyester running shorts and striped eighties throw-back sweatband. My sister would match him step for step. Part of me was jealous of their athletic synchronicity.

I finished the first lap of the oval near the middle of the pack, then I started to feel the familiar contraction of muscle down my side. I jogged slowly through it, bracing against the discomfort. I finished my three laps about two-fifths of the way through the pack. I smiled triumphantly to myself as I finished my third lap and flopped down on the scratchy grass to catch my breath, wheezing hard. I hadn't come last. I hadn't walked. I hadn't embarrassed myself on the first day of sport.

'Oi!' Mr Spencer yelled towards the group of us flopped down on the grass at the edge of the finishing line. 'Stretch! You have to stretch before you sit!' He moved over towards us and scanned the group till his eyes rested on me.

'You! Clarkey!' he said.

'Me?'

'I said Clarkey, didn't I? You Cecelia's sister?'

'Yes.'

'Hmmph.' He looked disappointed. 'You usually run faster than that?'

'No, sir.'

'Never?'

'Not really, sir!'

'You were running as fast as you could?' He looked incredulous. 'We'll have to fix that up. Must be in there somewhere. Why don't you come to running group with your sister? We'll train you up.'

I stared back at him. I'd just run faster than I ever had before. I was pretty sure I couldn't *go* any faster. 'I'm not a runner, sir. I mean, I don't like running that much.'

Spencer looked at me, perplexed.

'Your sister,' he said, 'she's going to be a champion, Clarkey. Runs like the wind. It's in the blood. You folks are built for it!'

The rest of the class was listening now. Two kids who'd known me in primary school giggled dubiously. Others looked bored by the conversation. I picked up the bottom of my t-shirt, lowered my forehead to it and wiped away the sweat.

'Okay, grade seven, back over to the school oval. We'll get out the hockey sticks. C'mon! Get to your feet! Quickly! And mind yourselves crossing the road!'

'It's true, you know,' one of the boys walking behind me whispered. 'My brother went to state championships last year. With your sister, I mean. The boys call her the Black Flash . . .' He suddenly looked sheepish. 'Behind her back, I mean. Not to her face. Don't tell her that.'

In the showers, I turned Spencer's words over in my mind. Maybe it was really there, in my muscles and my bones somehow – that speed – and I just had to unlock it. When my dad watched the athletics championships on television, lots of the runners were black: Jamaicans, Kenyans, African Americans. What if I just needed coaching? I imagined myself, my legs moving in a long and steady stride, my breath even as my sneakers thudded the bitumen. I imagined hitting the streets with the kind of grace my sister did. Doing something a *real* black person could do. Actually becoming like Flo Jo.

At the dinner table that evening, I waited until there was a lull in the conversation. 'I'd like to start going to running group in the mornings too,' I announced as casually as I could manage.

Dad stared at me over his dessert bowl. He always brought a frozen cheesecake home on Wednesday evenings after his squash game. It was a kind of ritual. The cheesecake was one of my most favourite things in the world: creamy and biscuity, and always still half frozen when we ate it. Dad's eyes sparkled as he chewed, as if he was trying hard not to smirk.

'Of course you can,' said Mum, shooting a disappointed look in his direction. 'We leave at about seven-thirty in the morning, though.'

'Okay. I'll be ready.'

In the car, on the way to my first running group session, Cecelia glared angrily out of her window. I pretended not to notice her annoyance. This was my sister's terrain, and I knew it. But something inside of me believed I could do it. That I could be as talented on the sports field as she was, if I only applied myself.

There were about fifteen other kids there for the training session when we arrived.

'Clarkey!' Mr Spencer nodded, businesslike, at Cecelia. His eyes moved cautiously over to me. 'Clarkey,' he repeated.

He moved his gaze to encompass the rest of the group. 'Okay, let's go! No stragglers, eh?'

We jogged, all in a line, to the oval across the road from the school. Mr Spencer herded us to a steep grass embankment.

'Up the hill twenty times and down the hill twenty times!' he yelled. 'If you finish early, jog on the spot. What are you all waiting for? C'mon!'

The other running group regulars started to run up the hill. I followed slowly.

After hill training, there were squats and sprints. Then Mr Spencer led us to a set of knee-high metal benches.

'Twenty steps on each leg.'

The other kids began stepping up onto the bench, one foot up, then the other. One foot down, then the other. I stood staring at the bench. Cecelia looked over at me sympathetically, like she was about to say something.

'C'mon, little Clarkey!' Mr Spencer called. 'It's in the blood!'

I raised one foot, and levered myself slowly up onto the bench, panting and wheezing.

———————

Every fortnight, Mr Spencer would schedule a timed run. Instead of our usual training session, we'd run the actual cross country course to chart our progress and see if our times had improved. Our new times would be tacked up on the leaderboard outside the sports staffroom. The leaderboard listed the top thirty running times from each age group across the whole school.

Slowly, over the course of two or three months, I worked my way onto the leaderboard, into place number thirty. I sat there, in thirtieth place, week after week after week. Five seconds would be shaved off my time one fortnight. Then eight seconds the next. Then nothing the next. But despite my religious attendance at running group every Monday, Wednesday and Friday morning, I never managed to crack the top twenty-nine.

One morning, after running group, I stood staring up at the Under 14s leaderboard. Mr Spencer walked up behind me.

'It's not happening, is it, Clarkey?' he asked forlornly.

'No.' There wasn't much else to say, really.

'You're really trying your hardest?'

'I am.'

'Well I never.' The man sounded genuinely perplexed. He rested a hand gently on my shoulder, as if he didn't want me to realise what a dismal failure my life was going to be.

———————

There was something about running group that kept me going back, even when it became clear I would never be the runner my sister was, even after Mr Spencer began to imply that I was holding the group back and should perhaps take up another pursuit. I actually began to revel in the almost unbearable pain of it. The bursting lungs. The crippling stitches. The burning away from my mind of everything else that was happening in my life for that hour and a half spent pounding the streets. I began to wonder if this was what Cecelia felt, too, when she sprinted; if this was partly why my sister ran. To get the hell away from this place. To grow wings for that brief but all-encompassing moment.

It was the first time I'd seriously pondered the probability that there were separate, but parallel, schoolyard hells in which me, Cecelia, Bronson, and any other child of difference existed. That folklore way of humming a scale. This is how it riffed.

15.

NEAR THE START of the year, in grade eight history class, our teacher Miss Cooke shoved a VHS tape into the clunky metal television she'd wheeled to the front of the room. She fast-forwarded through the advertisements until she reached the news broadcast she'd taped from television at the end of the last school year. The Australian prime minister, Paul Keating, was flanked by an Aboriginal man playing a didgeridoo. The wind danced about in the prime minister's thinning hair. The teacher fast-forwarded a bit more. This is how it happened: the tell of it sure. Facts just so: that West Indian way of spreading folklore. Gasps and guffaws in all the right places, or else what's a story for.

'I brought this in because we've been discussing Australian history, and I'm keen to know what everyone in the class thinks about it.' Miss Cooke seemed excited as she bustled about making sure the screen was angled so we could all see it.

She pressed play, and moved to the side of the room.

'*It begins, I think, with that act of recognition,*' the prime minister said into the microphone in his familiar orator's voice. The camera panned over the huge outdoor crowd, which buzzed with anticipation. I could feel the sense of excitement. '*Recognition that it was we who did the dispossessing. We took the traditional lands and smashed the traditional way of life.*'

I stopped tapping my pencil against the desk, and straightened in my seat.

'*We brought the diseases. The alcohol. We committed the murders. We took the children from their mothers. We practised discrimination and exclusion.*'

On the screen, cheers rang out from the crowd. The prime minister's face was sombre; pained.

'*It was our ignorance and our prejudice. And our failure to imagine these things being done to us . . .*'

Miss Cooke pressed pause and stepped in front of the television, excitement gleaming in her green eyes. 'This speech marks a turning point in Australia's history. After everything we've studied so far, I'm really interested to know what you all think.' She rested one hand on her hip. I liked Miss Cooke and the way she taught us Australian history. In addition to what was in the history textbooks we studied from – which were old and dog-eared and looked like they'd been in the history storeroom for about fifty billion years – she had also told us about Eddie Mabo, the Murray Islander who'd challenged the Australian government for native title of his people's land and won. Miss Cooke told us that the idea of *terra nullius*, the presumption that Australia had belonged to no-one when Captain Cook arrived, had been judged incorrect in the High Court. She confirmed that what Mrs Hird had taught us in those grade three bicentenary classes was as bizarre as I'd suspected.

'I think it's good.' A red-haired girl with thick glasses raised her hand as she spoke. 'I mean, I think the recognition of what happened was good. But still, it was, like, our *ancestors* who did it. Not *us*.'

'You think it's *good*. Seriously? Are you for real?' Greg Adams spluttered loudly, from where he was sitting at the back of the classroom, scratching words into the desk with his geometry compass.

The rest of the class turned in their seats.

'Nobody gives a shit about the abos. Except maybe blackie over there.' He flicked a thumb in my direction. 'We should have wiped them all out when we had the fucken chance.'

'GET OUT!' Our teacher's voice cracked with rage. She pointed a stick of chalk at Greg. 'Get out of my classroom, *right this minute!*'

Greg Adams gathered his bag and school folder and walked towards the door. Just before he got to the doorway, he smirked over at me. 'Abo,' he mouthed, then left the room.

Greg Adams was solidly built, with mean, piercing eyes. He would have been twice my weight and was at least a head taller than me. Greg Adams called me *dirty* and *disgusting*. He recoiled when I came near him, in a deliberately exaggerated way. Greg Adams hated wogs, and chinks, and niggers, and abos, and curry munchers. His hatred was wide, and loud, and vicious, and *entitled*. His hatred knew no bounds.

Mr Chandra, our grade eight maths teacher, was a small, thin man with a slim pencil moustache and a haircut that made him look like an overgrown boy. His black chinos were always carefully pleat-ironed down the front of each leg. He wore collared shirts in white and purple checks or bright green leaf print. Mr Chandra was patient, and friendly, and jovial. Greg Adams hated him.

'Sir, what did you say?' Greg often asked, all mock-innocence and confusion.

The class fell silent, aware of the charade that was starting.

'Calcalatta,' Mr Chandra responded. His tone was calm, but I recognised the weariness, the carefully constrained exasperation.

'Pardon, sir?'

'I said please take out your calcalattas.'

'Take out our *what*?'

It was a game Greg Adams loved to play with all of the teachers who had foreign accents: Mrs Pang, who taught geography; Mrs Kim, our science teacher; and Mr Chandra.

'You know what I am talking about, Greg.' Mr Chandra looked Greg dead in the face.

'Actually, I *don't* know what you're talking about. What's a cal-car-latt-err? That isn't even English.'

Another kid once attempted to intervene. 'Cut it out, Greg. You know he means *calculator*.'

'I *don't* know what he means.' Greg ran a hand over his acne-scarred face and millimetre-short buzz-cut in mock-despair. 'My dad says you curry munchers shouldn't be able to teach us if you can't even speak English properly. It's a disgrace.'

The teachers' reactions differed. Sometimes they would ignore Greg's commentary. Other times they would send him outside. They tended to resist this latter course of action: experience indicated direct confrontation was a large part of his objective.

———

My friend Selina turned in her seat one maths lesson and tried to reason with Greg as he started in on our teacher again. 'Surely you have some ethnic mix in your family?'

'French and Scottish – that's it,' said Greg proudly. 'White people should be separated from everyone else. People who aren't white make me sick just looking at them. I can't help it, they just do.'

In covert moments – while Selina and I were waiting at the crowded stop after school to board the bus back to Kellyville, or sitting in a quiet corner of the playground, Greg Adams would approach. As he sauntered past, he'd hawk a huge glob of phlegm to the back of his throat, then spit it in my direction.

Greg Adams loudly ranked the girls in our class from one to eleven on his Fuck Chart. He said he couldn't even put me at the end of the list because *animals* didn't count. Greg Adams said that would be bestiality. Greg Adams said the only way black chicks got fucked was gang-banged with the lights turned off, and even then you'd have to be super desperate, and use ten condoms so you didn't get AIDS. And then Greg Adams and his friends laughed, and laughed, and laughed.

I stood in the principal's office, hysterically hiccupping sobs.

I lost count of how many times.

There was a bit of wall behind the principal's desk – a small area about thirty centimetres by twenty – where the paint was peeling from the white top coat through to the older layer underneath. Through the blur of tears it looked as if the wall was eating itself away: slowly eroding, the white top layer curling up to reveal the browning tea-stain-on-saucer paint beneath it. The pattern of it made this section of the wall look like vintage lace: like abandonment, and trauma, and heartache. It reminded me of Miss Havisham from *Great Expectations*: of her yellowing wedding gown, a life of bitterness, a life unlived. I got to know the pattern of it, of this one spot on the wall that I stared at. Twenty years later, I could map that peel.

'Maxine, I can't help you if you won't tell me what he said.'

My chest heaved up and down. 'He said . . . Greg said I . . .' A rasping sound was coming from my chest. It sounded guttural: muffled by uniform and flesh. My throat was closing up.

'He said things . . . about . . .'

'Do you want to write it down? Here, write down what he said.' The principal pushed a lined pad of paper and a black biro over the desk towards me.

I stared at the pad of paper. 'No . . . I can't . . . I don't want to write it down.' Not my hand, moving across the paper, inscribing what he'd said to me. I couldn't.

'He's trying to wind you up. It's just a little bit of nonsense. Don't give him the satisfaction, Maxine.' The principal slowly adjusted his tie, as if my very presence in his office somehow made him uncomfortable. Tiny beads of sweat had formed on his forehead.

I returned to class: shuffled back into my seat with my red-rimmed eyes cast down towards the pilled grey carpet, shoulders bowed, folded into myself.

'Bet she's gone and dobbed to a teacher or something.'

'Yeah. She went to the principal, and he gave her one of the bananas he keeps for her in his bottom drawer.' Greg Adams and his mates made monkey noises, just softly enough that the teacher wouldn't hear them.

Every time Greg Adams was reprimanded, the bullying got worse.

Sometimes, he delegated the task to his friends.

Maxine Beneba Clarke

Greg's mate Lachlan Jones also had a game he liked to play, and I was the lucky person he played it with. He stuck his leg out every time I walked past, with the aim of tripping me up. When I tried to get to my seat in class, or onto the school bus, or down the aisle in assembly, Lachlan Jones strategically placed himself where I couldn't avoid him, in the ultimate game of dodge.

Even the times I didn't fall, or stumble, or get pushed, Greg and Lachlan and their coterie of loutish mates still found the whole exercise amusing, shrieking with laughter and applauding each other's efforts.

'Who wants to get through?' Lachlan asked me, his tall lanky frame blocking the entrance to the girls toilets. I looked down at his feet. His white Adidas socks were covered in blue fluff, like they'd accidentally been put through a dark wash. His sneakers looked as though they'd been painted with white Scuff Stuff leather cleaner, but you could still see through to the cracked, worn grey leather underneath.

'Let me past.' I tried to stand my ground.

'Who wants to come past?'

'I do.'

'Who wants to come past?' Lachlan pushed his face right into mine: so close that I could smell the tuna sandwich on his breath.

'I do.'

'And what are you?'

'Let me past!' My bladder was almost ready to let go.

'What are you?'

'A blackie.' I wanted it to be over. It didn't matter what I said, as long as it ended.

There was a place I went to, inside my head. A red–black pulsing place that was both dark and brilliant. As if I'd closed my

154

eyes at the height of a sparkling summer day and turned my face directly up towards the sun. From this other-side place, I would hear myself, saying whatever I needed to.

'That's right. Say it again.'

'A blackie.'

Only then did Lachlan Jones step aside. Only after I said it. Then he and his friends walked away, hooting.

What are you?

What are you?

What are you?

I always knew.

I always knew what answer to give.

I knew.

I knew exactly what I was.

I was Coon. I was Jungle Bunny. I was Monkey Girl. I was Gorilla. I was Lubra Lips. I was Nigger. I was Blackie, or Golliwog. I was Tar Baby. I was Dog Turd. I was Ape, Baboon or Big Lips. I was Steel Wool, Fuzzy Wuzzy or Camel Girl. I was Choco, Darkie or Jigaboo. I was Donkey Kong. King Kong. Sambo. They called me Knuckle Dragger. Girl Dingo. Kaffir. Or sometimes Cockroach. I was Brownie, or Africana, or often just plain Nostrils. I was Niggie. I was Sooty, Boong, Thick Lips.

Somewhere along the line we give up counting.

Somewhere along the line, we just give in.

Somewhere along the line, we stop reporting.

Somewhere along the line, we die a little.

———

At night, when nobody was watching, I tried to claw my way out of my skin. At first, I didn't know I was doing it. It wasn't even a conscious thing. I would wake in the morning with dried blood crusted on my fingers; a handful of angry pink welts on my face where my nails had dug in furiously. The behaviour became habitual. My hands would flutter unthinkingly around my face, fingernails absent-mindedly peeling back layers of flesh and skin. The healed marks would scar over: fade to dark, uneven blotches. Distressed black and grey marks clustered on my chin, and cheeks.

This is how it broke me.

This is how I coped.

My father cut my nails right down to the quick: below the white distal fold, right down to the nail plate. He cut them so short the exposed pomegranate skin beneath my fingernails stung like paper cuts.

I didn't know how to stop clawing at myself.

I didn't know how to tell my parents that I didn't know how to stop.

I was sent to the school counsellor's office. Her room was small, bare and claustrophobic. To reach it, you went into the glass-walled school office building and climbed a spiral staircase to the top floor. Everyone in the playground could see you being led up there. Within five minutes, everyone in the school knew you were *fucked in the head.*

A kid named Timothy Jenkins had climbed the stairs to the counsellor's office at the very start of grade seven. He went up there twice a week, on Wednesdays and Fridays. Timothy had been in my grade, but not in any of my classes. I'd never spoken to him, but I'd still heard about him going to the counsellor's office. Everyone knew. Timothy Jenkins had scars all the way up the inside of one of his arms, and long curly hair. He sometimes wore nail polish. Greg Adams and Lachlan Jones talked about him. They said he was a freak and a sissy.

Whenever I saw Timothy in the corridors, he'd walked so slowly, cautiously, like he knew there was something fragile inside him that could shatter at any moment. When term four started, Timothy hadn't come back to school. There'd been no announcement or anything. He'd just disappeared. Some kid in the grade above us said he'd seen Timothy at the local skating rink, and he wasn't Timothy anymore, he was Tina.

The school counsellor was a large sweet-faced woman with slender always-waggling fingers and an annoying way of constantly clearing her throat.

'Is there anything else going on?' she asked me. 'Other than a little bit of teasing?'

I stared at her, then looked around the obsessively tidy room. I thought about Timothy, with the scars up his arm, who was probably now Tina. I wondered if she'd said the words *a little bit of teasing* to him as well.

'Yes – I have an eating disorder,' I said. A girl on *Degrassi Junior High*, Kathleen, had an eating disorder. I'd decided an eating disorder was the kind of problem pretty white girls had. The kind of problem the counsellor could possibly solve.

'What kind of eating disorder?' The counsellor's demeanour changed. She became more businesslike, as if here was an actual real problem.

'I'm bulimic.'

'Okay.' She wrote something down on her notepad.

'Do you . . . do you make yourself vomit?'

'All the time,' I said forlornly.

The school counsellor looked up at me suddenly, pen hovering, as she took in my healthy size twelve frame.

'I need to ask you, Maxine, are you *serious* about this?'

'I don't have an eating disorder,' I conceded. 'That was just a joke. I'm sorry. I know I shouldn't joke about things like that but . . . I think I'm pregnant.' Spike on *Degrassi Junior High* was pregnant. Spike had a crazy punk hairdo and didn't give a fuck what anyone thought.

'Maxine, this isn't a joke,' the counsellor reprimanded me. 'If you don't need to be here, there are other kids who might actually need my help.'

The next time a note was sent for me to go down to the office to visit the school counsellor, I excused myself from the classroom and went to read in the library instead.

At home, I would lock the bathroom door and stare at myself in the mirror, stare at the small bruises on my face.

At school, the teasing took a foreseeable turn.

'What's wrong with your face?' Lachlan Jones asked, blocking my way into the library.

'Nothing.'

'I said what's wrong with your face?'

'Nothing. Let me past.'

'You have AIDS,' he said forcefully. 'Say you have AIDS and I'll let you through, monkey girl.'

My mother was usually the queen of stalwartness, but when she looked at me, I could see the alarm in her eyes. Like she knew there was an unfathomable brokenness somewhere inside of me, to which my skin was bearing witness.

16.

EVEN THOUGH THERE was a bus stop directly around the corner from my house, on weekday mornings I would walk the fifteen minutes to Selina's and catch the bus with her up at the Kellyville shops, around the corner from her house. We would stuff our skirt pockets with Milky Ways and Nougat Honey Logs, bought from the local milk bar with change I'd nicked from Mum's purse.

We'd become inseparable, Selina and I, in that swear-on-your-life, spit-sister way only teenage girls can connect. On weekends we'd lock ourselves into her bedroom or mine, and we'd write. We'd create characters and plots and other worlds to weave ourselves into. We'd write notes to each other – endless, hopelessly angst-ridden notes – confiding in each other about our hopes and dreams and despairs. I never wrote about the racism in those letters, though. The trauma was too great, too consuming. Too unmentionable.

Selina was a serious asthmatic, and in grade eight her health took a turn for the worst. Her absences became more frequent, and without another body to walk the corridors beside me, I felt utterly exposed.

At fourteen, the playground was still very much divided into boy and girl cliques. There was a handful of other girls at school I was on friendly terms with, but nowhere near the kind of friendship Selina and I had. Nowhere near the kind of friendship a fourteen-year-old girl needs through the stretch in her bones of her hips filling out. Through the training bras, and moving up a cup size each year. Nowhere near the kind of friend a teenager needs to help her navigate orthodontic braces, and how best to shoplift pink Gillette for Women razors; to work out tampons, and pimples, and that awful period pain that ached in every fibre of your flesh. Nowhere near the kind of friend who knew you when you weren't even sure you knew yourself.

Underneath my increasingly adult acceptance of my difference, there was still the misfit remnants of a longing to fit in. Never did I feel this more keenly than the times Selina was away from school ill, and I navigated the schoolyard alone.

The grade eight girls weren't as vicious as Greg Adams and his mates were, not as openly and violently racist. But there was an awful, aching silence about them: that hurtful bystander complicity I still remembered from the BMX track when I was back in primary school.

'Don't be slack, Greg!' one of them might reprimand, laughing, as the boys pushed me to the edge. But by and large, most of them turned their heads the other way. Even those whose houses I frequented, those on my weekend tennis team or who sat next to me at band practice, didn't want to know. They disengaged. Theirs was a silence most deafening.

The general playground pecking order made *Lord of the Flies* seem like a tea party. Among the girls, it was *Looking for Alibrandi* meets *Hating Alison Ashley* meets *Puberty Blues*. Not an easy place for a book-geek black girl like me.

The cool girls Banana-Boated their long, lean summer legs, moisturising them to oil-slick shininess. The cool girls wore long knee socks scrunched down around slim ankles like leg-warmers. They rolled their tartan skirts at the waist until the hem sat well above the knee. They sat up the back of the oval, near the agriculture field, at lunchtime. Up the back, there was heavy breathing, hands under skirts, unhooked bras.

For awkwardly ordinary nineties girls in mid-adolescence, the swan metamorphosis still seemed within reach. There were one or two grade eight girls who'd proved it was possible: knock-kneed buck-toothed, freckle-faced things who emerged from mousy pigtails, braces and growth spurts as if they'd just walked off the set of a Pantene commercial. These precious few fuelled every misfit's fantasy.

By grade eight, the wake-up-white prayers of my childhood had been well and truly reality-checked. I knew it would take an awful lot for broad-nosed, coffee-toned, B-cup, study-freak me to make the grass-greener leap. But I was still convinced there were things I could do which would bring me closer, at least, to popularity.

Towards the end of grade eight, I started pleading with my mother to let me chemically straighten my hair. I knew I could never have the flickable blonde masses of the more popular of my classmates. But perhaps I could get a blunt-cut Salt-N-Pepa-style fringe, or a ponytail that hung down my back like Rudy from *The Cosby Show*. I hated the unruly afro-frizz which escaped from my stumpy ponytail after sport, or swimming, or just unthinkingly running my hand over my head.

One day, through the sparse but highly effective black grape-vine, we heard about Greek Charlie. Greek Charlie was an up-and-coming hairdresser with his own salon in Granville. He was fast developing a reputation for being able to get black hair *Chinese straight*. From the moment I heard a family friend whisper these words to my mother, I knew that *Chinese straight* was exactly what I needed to turn my life around. A torturous months-long pestering campaign later, it was agreed that the salon visit could function as an early birthday present.

That West Indian way, of spinning a tale. This is how it happened. Sitting in the salon chair, the smell of the straightener so potent I could barely breathe, a crawling sensation spreading across my scalp.

'It feels a bit funny,' I said.

'Good,' Charlie said triumphantly, flicking a hand in the air to dismiss my discomfort. 'That means it's working, darling.'

The sensation got stronger. I tried to sit still, staring back at my reflection in the mirror. *Chinese straight*, I repeated to myself.

I remembered back in grade three, when my hair had been trimmed so short I wasn't able to fit it into a ponytail; how I'd worn it in a short afro; how that kid had brought her golliwog in for show-and-tell, and the nickname had stuck. I gritted my teeth against the burning.

Once, in grade seven, the elastic band holding my ponytail had broken in the middle of class, my entire afro springing free. *Oh my god, she looks like she just stuck her finger in an electrical socket. Fuzzy wuzzy. Scarecrow. Steel wool. Toilet brush.*

The searing pain became unbearable. 'It's burning now,' I said finally, giving in to the pain. 'It's *burning*.'

'It's supposed to, darling,' Charlie said from over at the basin where he'd started a shampoo.

'I don't like it. Take it off, please. Take it off!'

'Just a few more minutes, sweetie. It'll be worth it.' Charlie poured conditioner into his hand. To take my mind off the burning, he started small talking. 'You got a special occasion coming up, honey?'

'Not really. Well, I mean, my friend has a pool party tomorrow.'

Charlie stared at me in the mirror. 'You're going swimming, after this *magic*? Oh, darling, why didn't you come after the party? You'll have to keep your hair dry for two weeks after this.'

By the time Charlie massaged the neutraliser into my hair, the damage was done. On the back of my head, in the centre of my newly straightened hair, was a round pink patch the size of a fifty-cent coin where the chemicals had burned clean through both hair and skin.

———————

The birthday girl was midway up the playground popularity ladder, and spent every second at school desperately trying to grab the next rung. I was on her weekend sports team, and she'd made it clear when she delivered the invitation it was out of obligation.

'My mum said I'd better invite you.'

I didn't care that I wasn't really wanted, or that Selina hadn't been invited; I was going anyway. Before the pool party, my mother gently rubbed mascara over the pink fleshy patch at the back of my head to conceal the wound.

I looked on, from the pool deck, at the game of volleyball unfolding in the water.

'Maxine, don't you want to go in the water?' the birthday girl's mother asked, perplexed. She was sitting on a deckchair nearby, vaguely supervising proceedings.

'No, it's okay.'

'Go on, get in! It's such a hot day.'

It was tempting. I swatted a fly away from my legs, thought about the mascara slathered onto my scalp, the effort Charlie had gone to. The cost of the salon visit.

'Can't you swim?' The woman adjusted her bathing suit and glanced at my shrieking classmates.

'I can swim,' I said defensively.

'Oh. *That* time of the month, darling?' She threw a sympathetic glance my way.

'No!' I said, mortified, as one of the girls walked past us, giggling, to fetch her towel.

'Then what's the problem?'

'My hair . . .' I said, reluctantly, knowing even as I opened my mouth it was a bad idea. 'I had it done yesterday. I'm not supposed to wash it for two weeks.'

The woman stared at me. 'Is that a joke?' she asked, half smiling. 'You're not supposed to wash your hair for *two weeks*?' she repeated, loudly enough for all my classmates to hear. 'Won't it be . . . *dirty*?' She screwed up her nose.

I took a deep breath, not knowing where to start blacksplaining the difference between Anglo hair and afro hair. Incredulous tittering had already started down in the pool.

'Oh my god. She is *so* weird.'

'That's gross.'

'Seriously, why did you even invite her? It's embarrassing.'

I imagined turning up for school the next day, the rumours

already having spread about how I refused to go in the pool because I didn't like to have clean hair.

I stood up. 'Actually, I think I will go for a swim.' I kicked off my thongs, slipped out of my denim cut-offs, waded into the pool. I took a breath, and dived under the water.

As I surfaced, I caught sight of the rest of the kids madly scrambling out of the pool.

'We don't feel like being in the pool anymore,' the party girl said, smiling down at me as they grabbed their towels and headed inside.

I stood in the centre of the pool, staring at the decidedly frizzy ends of wet hair hanging in my eyes.

'Oh my goodness!' The host's mum suddenly sprang up from her chair. 'Are you okay, Maxine? Did you hit your head? There's . . . there's a gash at the back of your head. Kids? Kids! I think she's hurt herself!'

The pool party marked the end of longing-to-belong, destroyed the final remnants of caring-what-they-thought. My naive idea that things could change had been firmly turned around. Standing out the front of the party girl's house in my damp frizzy-again hair and yellow halter-neck swimmers, waiting for my mum to pick me up, I had at last come to realise that I didn't even *like* most of these girls I'd somehow come to idolise. That if my best friend wasn't around, I preferred my own company. The realisation was enormous. It was sad, and tragic, and depressing. It was comforting, glorious, and freeing. It was bittersweet.

When I gather the threads in my fingers, this is how they weave.

17.

THE MARGINS BETWEEN events have blended and shifted in the tell of it. There's that folklore way West Indians have of weaving a tale: facts just so, gasps and guffaws in all the right places, because after all, what else is a story for?

Fourteen or fifteen is that age where all the world seems to happen outside of your home. Where what matters most are notes passed, and boys kissed, and clothes worn, and whatever dubious piece of sex advice *Cosmopolitan* magazine or *Dolly* Doctor is dishing out that week, even though you're not even close to doing it yet.

Somehow, family life faded to the background. It was there, as it always had been – there in a structural sense – but it seemed to just fill up the gaps between *actual things happening*. I was vaguely aware of goings-on in Bronson and Cecelia's lives. Aware enough to realise that on some level, each of us was fighting our own private war.

Bronson's room was always a disaster zone: wet bath towels in heaps on the floor, papers and school books strewn all over the place, cassette tapes in small piles, plates full of toast crumbs.

No matter how many times Mum got him to clean his room, a few hours later it would somehow have reverted back to its dishevelled state. At just eleven, Bronson had already embraced sloppy-teenage-boy mode with a determination that continually frustrated my parents.

One Saturday afternoon, Mum called sharply to my brother, 'Bronson! I found this in your room. Can you please explain to me what it is?' My mother's curt tone caused Cecelia and me to also come running.

In Mum's hand was a crumpled note, typed on the primary school's letterhead.

'I don't know.' My brother sullenly stuck out his bottom lip.

'Well, I found the envelope too. It was addressed to me and your father.' Mum looked at my brother pointedly.

'It's just some stupid letter.' Bronson shrugged.

'A *stupid letter* inviting me to go up to the school to *discuss your behaviour*.' Mum was still staring at him, shocked. 'What does *launching foreign objects at a teacher* mean?'

I could see the school principal's signature at the bottom of the letter: Mr Parkinson, who'd become my grade six arch nemesis, who'd made me stand against The Wall at least once a week for my entire final term of primary school. The sight of his lavishly embellished sign-off made me feel sick.

My brother smirked. 'I just threw jellybeans at her. From the balcony. When she was on playground duty.'

'Wipe that *smirk* off your face. Why would you do something like that?'

I thought about Mrs Hird, and her response to Derek harassing me in grade five. *Blackie. Well, that's what you are.* I could remember the fierce hatred I'd harboured towards her. I knew *exactly* why Bronson might *do something like that.*

'And what is this on the letter here?' Mum shook the crumpled piece of paper in my brother's unremorseful face.

'Snot.'

'*I beg your pardon?*'

'I opened it, I read it, and I blew my nose on it.'

'You *what*?!' Mum stared at him, her mouth open.

Cecelia and I were in stitches now, lolling about the kitchen, laughing our heads off.

'Go to your room right now!' yelled Mum. 'You just *wait* until your father gets home.'

Bronson shrugged his shoulders, and headed down the hallway.

'And you two!' Mum scolded Cecelia and me. 'You should know better than to encourage him like that.'

My sister and I stifled our giggles and walked sheepishly back to our respective bedrooms.

Cecelia, meanwhile, had hit sixteen, and like all other sixteen-year-olds, she was chasing certain freedoms. Her handsome new athletics coach, Martin, was twenty years old. She spent a lot of time training with him. When he asked her to go shopping for running sneakers one afternoon after school, my sister went, despite my parents forbidding the excursion. All hell broke loose when my sister walked through the door after the outing. My mother's fury reverberated around the house.

These were the other lives playing out on the periphery of mine. With all of us in, or approaching, adolescence, we spent much less time together. We'd been used to driving miles across the country in our family's beat-up Ford Falcon in the school holidays: towels spread across the vinyl back seat to stop our thighs from being scorched. We'd always ended up at daggy affordable family holiday destinations: Mollymook, The Entrance, the Western Plains Zoo, Woy Woy, Jenolan Caves, Canberra. There'd be squabbling, and yelling, and back-seat tears; on-the-road games of I-spy. There'd be barbecues, and McDonald's, and dodgy caravans or motels. There'd be the locals, gaping open-mouthed at us, in whatever small coastal or country town we'd drifted into; storekeepers with caricature drawls who asked us warily where we'd *blown in from*.

Those close-quarters family times were drawing to an end now, mostly due to the whining protestations of us children. But in September of grade nine, a chicken pox epidemic flared up at the school Cecelia and I went to. It hit our household for six, attacking us teens without mercy. The whole family went into lockdown together.

I barely remember anything from the first week I was down with chicken pox. Sweating fevers. Begging for Panadol. Endlessly pouring calamine lotion onto small balls of cotton wool and dabbing at my spots with them. Descending into a strange and disturbing delirium. I remember Selina dropping by one day, standing in the hallway trying to talk to me, because she wasn't allowed to come any closer. Me mumbling incoherently in her general direction.

The chicken pox virus made its way into Bronson's left eye, a small red itchy lump forming on the surface of his eyeball, which would affect his vision for the rest of his life. On my own sensitive skin, the red spots did their usual thing: turning to watery pustules, which crusted over and turned to scabs, which eventually dropped off, leaving faint pink circles.

Well after us kids returned to our respective schoolyards, the light pink circles remained. They itched incessantly – across my back and shoulders, on my neck and ears, on my legs and stomach and arms. It was as if the disease had never left my system.

Then the small, flat pink circles began to grow.

Over the course of several months, they rose up out of my skin. At first they were subtle indentations, like braille. Then they puffed up higher and higher, grew hard and shiny, like half-peanuts glued all over my body. The unbearable itch of them seemed nerve-deep – not the surface irritation of a mosquito bite or rash. My chicken pox scars itched, and I scratched. And they itched, and I scratched. And they grew, and grew.

I found myself, again, in a dermatologist's office. It was a different place from the one I had visited when the faded watermarks of vitiligo had encroached on my life some six years earlier, but there was that same anthropological way the doctor examined me: as if I were some kind of throwback species. The soft, patronising voice. The stark waiting room. Lights shone onto my skin. Magnifiers peered through. The taking of an illustrated medical encyclopaedia off the shelf.

'Have you ever heard of hypertrophic or keloid scarring?' The doctor swung around in his chair to show us the picture in the book.

'Yes, I have,' my mother confessed quietly, as if her worst fears had been confirmed.

The doctor cleared his throat, and read a passage from the book out loud. '*A sharply elevated, irregularly shaped, progressively enlarging scar, due to excessive collagen formation in the corium during connective tissue repair. A benign tumour. A nodular, movable, non-encapsulated,* mass of hyperplastic scar tissue. Can be tender, and frequently painful. Most commonly occurring in blacks.'

My mind started wandering. A wild panic set in.

'. . . basically just a large scar . . . the body doesn't know when to stop producing tissue . . .'

I drifted in and out of the conversation, sitting dead still with my hands folded in my lap.

'You know those African tribes you sometimes see on television documentaries, or in the *National Geographic*?' the doctor said, barely concealing his intrigue. 'The ones with those scarification marks all over them, little raised puffy dots? That's keloid scarring. That's probably where this aspect of your skin originates from.'

Those African tribes. Where your skin originates from. The population of Jamaica, like those inhabiting most of the West Indies, are the descendants of African slaves. Blackie. That's what you are. What are you? What are you? Blackie. That's right. That pulsing red-black place inside my head. *Transported inside the lower deck of a slave ship.*

As my mother and the dermatologist discussed potential treatments, my mind turned cartwheels. *Most commonly occurring in blacks.* My colour was again betraying me; my history asserting itself.

'Cortisone injections . . .' the doctor was saying. 'It's up to you and your daughter, Mrs Clarke, but the newer and softer the scar is, the more chance the injections have of minimising the scar.'

'What do you want to do, Maxine?' My mum looked over at me.

I stared at the spiral-bound day-to-an-opening calendar on the doctor's desk, willing my vision not to blur over, willing the tears not to fall.

'. . . could do a couple of them today and see how we go . . . or else wait and see . . .'

The scar tissue wasn't soft, I knew that. The scar tissue was shiny and hard – like there was bone in the centre of it. I had run my fingers over the pockmarks enough times to know that. While my mother and the doctor waited for me to make a decision, he moved his gaze to my face.

'What about your face, Maxine?' he said.

I shrugged, as if I wasn't sure what he was talking about.

'Are there particular times when something happens at home, and you do that to yourself?'

My mother shifted uncomfortably in her chair. We both knew what he was insinuating – that I had a troubled home life. That that kind of compulsive bruising could only be the result of a disturbed home environment. I hated the doctor for the pseudo-psychiatry he was engaging in – for making assumptions about my family. I wanted to swear at him, to smash his fancy medical equipment, scatter the sterile swabs and bandages all over the floor.

'Okay,' I said, desperate to change the topic. 'I'll have the injections today.'

The dermatologist rolled up the sleeves of his grey collared shirt, sterilised his hands at the sink, and drew some liquid into a small syringe.

'Take a deep breath in.'

It felt as if the needle was blunt. The thick scar tissue resisted. My entire body braced against the force of the needle as it punctured the knotted keloid on my shoulders, then the elongated scar in the centre of my back.

'Jeez, it's hard tissue in here,' the doctor said, seeming concerned as he wiped away the blood with cotton wool.

Tears rolled down my face. I continued crying while he taped soft white gauze over the small, burning tumours. I continued crying as we walked across the car park, my mum's hand resting on my shoulder. I sobbed all the way home.

———————

The keloid scarring wasn't like the vitiligo. It didn't sort itself out over time. The scars the dermatologist had test-injected itched, and grew, and itched, and grew, until they were double the size of the original keloids. Summer arrived, and I no longer wore singlets. In the sports changing rooms at school, I began dressing and undressing inside a stall. It was as if the scars were angry that they'd been disturbed; were livid at the poison which had been injected into them and were fighting against it. At night the disturbed tissue burned, hot and tight, on my back and shoulders. At the swimming pool, I wore a t-shirt on top of my costume.

'What happened to your neck?' asked Lachlan Jones as he walked behind me in the school corridor.

'She tried to cut her throat,' Greg Adams snickered. 'Should have used a sharper blade.'

Something had to give.

I knew *something had to give.*

This is how the melody changed: that folklore way, of twisting a tale.

Michael Callingham came along at exactly the right time. Mick entered my life as if from nowhere, but really he'd been lurking on the outskirts, waiting in the wings all that time. That West Indian way, of spinning a tale. This is how it hummed.

When my mum heard a local youth club was starting up in Kellyville, she enthusiastically put the word out among the other parents she knew. The non-denominational youth group was to run on Friday evenings, from six till nine, in The Barn – which was just that – an enormous abandoned barn up the top of Hectare Street, on the grounds owned by the Catholic parish and primary school.

And so, one winter Friday night, sullen with apathy, Selina and I were unceremoniously delivered by my mother to the fledgling Kellyville Youth Club. The Barn stood in the middle of a large, empty field, next to the school grounds. The closest building was the parish residence, which was set further back on the block. There was no lighting in the sprawling field other than the dim lights of The Barn, which cast a blurry, golden glow for several metres around it, as well as inside over the wooden floorboards, exposed ceiling beams and rusty vestiges of old farm equipment that lay, skeletal, in the dark corners.

When we stepped inside, we were greeted by a petite young woman in her mid-twenties wearing tight denim jeans and a long knitted jumper, who introduced herself as Narelle.

Selina and I chatted with the handful of other teenagers in attendance. Narelle sat on a chair in the corner, with her head buried in a book. About an hour or so into the gathering, a clatter of loud footsteps approached the Barn. Three boys, who looked around sixteen or so, were standing in the doorway, shoulder to shoulder, surveying the group of us, casting long shadows into the dimly lit room.

'Hey!' said the tallest of them. He was rugby material this kid: tight muscles were visible beneath his hoodie and black jeans. 'I'm Kurt. This is Jed.' He gestured to the boy standing on his right, who was of medium height with slightly crooked teeth and a friendly, studious look about him. 'And this is Mick.' He gestured, finally, to the third boy.

The third boy wore a large khaki trench coat that came all the way down to his shins, over slightly grubby bootleg jeans. The third boy had wavy caramel-coloured hair that fell slightly over his forehead. The third boy had beautiful tanned skin and a brooding mysterious darkness in his hazel eyes. The third boy walked like he was floating: a casual gait that emphasised his slim hips and broad-but-not-too-broad shoulders. The third boy and his friends made their way over to where Selina and I were sitting.

'Hi.' I was nervous all of a sudden, stammering in a way I never had before, conscious of the almost-faded grey bruises on my face, the wisps of hair escaping from my plait. Dust shone in the dim shafts of light between us. 'This is, um . . . this is Selina. And I'm Maxine.'

'Hi, Maxine,' said Mick. 'We already know each other. You and I are *old friends*.' He grabbed the chair across from me, threw back the tails of his long coat and sat down.

'We do?'

'I'm Michael Callingham,' he said, as if that explained everything.

'Ah. We *do* know each other.' I laughed. 'It's been quite a while.'

He laughed too, and when he did, cute crinkles crow-footed at the outside corners of his eyes. He had an ever-so-slight underbite that made his grin look super cute: not quite goofy, but handsomely cheeky. He held out his hand for me to shake, and when I took it, he pulled me in a little closer to him. His *smell*. Rexona for Men. Rollies. Damp earth. He smelled good. *So* good. I'd never been quite this close to a boy before, except for my little brother, or that fateful time I tried to kiss Lewis

Stevens in grade two. I tore my eyes away from Mick. Selina was staring at me.

'We, uh, we used to play together . . . uh . . . when we were little,' I explained clumsily.

There was one veterinary service in Kellyville, operated by Mick's dad. The surgery was on the bottom floor of a large brick house on Windsor Road. Mick's large Catholic family – seven or so kids, mostly boys – lived on the top floor. Almost every time we drove past, which was almost any time we drove in or out of Kellyville, my mother would peel her eyes away from the road for a split second and glance over at their place with regret.

'We *really* should get in touch with the Callinghams again,' she'd say. 'They were so good to us when we first moved here. You kids used to play over there all the time.'

Mum had sent us kids to the local state primary school. The Callinghams had sent their kids to the Catholic school on the hill. Apart from the occasional hello when they bumped into each other at the local shops, life had taken over and our parents had simply lost contact.

Now here he was, Michael you-and-I-are-old-friends Callingham: sitting on his chair backwards, sneaking glances at me. Mick. With his James Dean way of walking, and his laughing eyes, and his intoxicating smell. His beautiful broodiness. It was the first time a boy had *really* been interested in me. Before this, I hadn't even really considered it a possibility. Mick was the first boy who'd looked at me like I was worth looking at. Like he didn't ever want to look away. I was a little confused about the whole thing. Mick could see what I looked like: he could *see* that I was black. But it was like he couldn't see it at all. Or perhaps

176

even more baffling, like he *did* see it, and he nevertheless *liked* what he saw.

Selina was busy talking to Mick's mate Jed.

'Should we go for a walk?' Kurt, the rugby-shouldered boy asked, in his booming voice. It quickly became clear he was the leader of the trio, who knew each other from primary school. We headed outside, the whole group of ten or so teenagers, leaving Narelle buried in her book.

Outside The Barn, we disappeared into the velvet darkness. It was difficult to see more than a few metres in front of my face. The group dispersed in all different directions. Mick grabbed my hand, and pulled me over to a deserted corner of the field. We dropped down on the slightly damp grass.

'So, how's your life been for the last, oh, ten years, Maxine?' he asked.

There it was, that way he said my name in almost every sentence, as if he liked the way it sounded. I heard a rustle in the darkness. Mick's cigarette lighter flared between us. He took a rollie out of his jeans pocket, lit it. Took a long drag, moved his head to the side and exhaled.

'You smoke?'

'Nah.'

'Good thing.' He took another long drag, held it in and spoke through the corner of his mouth. '*Terrible* habit.' He blew the smoke off to the side again.

I swooned.

We covered a lot of ground, that first night. Mick was a private school boy, at a prestigious Jesuit college in the heart of the city. We both played the trumpet in the school band. He was into jazz, and theatre, and had a lead role coming up in his high school's musical production of *Midsummer Night's Dream*. He stubbed out his rollie, grabbed my hand, and weaved his fingers through mine. We headed back to The Barn. By the time Selina and Jed came back, they were going steady as well.

———————

My mum stared at me in the rear-view mirror of the second-hand Nimbus she'd recently acquired in place of our clunky Falcon. 'How was the youth group?'

'Good.'

I could feel her eyes on me.

'Anyone else there you knew?'

'Oh, I met Michael . . . uh . . . Callingham,' I said, as if it had only just occurred to me to mention him.

'The vet's kid! What's he like now?'

'He seems . . . *nice*.' I kept my voice as casual as possible as we pulled into our driveway.

'You reckon you'll go back next week?'

'I don't know. Maybe. If Selina wants to go again,' I said, careful to sound as bored as possible.

Inside, I quietly closed the door of my bedroom, flopped down onto my bed and pushed my face hard into the pillow to muffle my excited squeal.

Michael Callingham came along at just the right time. He was clean – untainted by all of the horrible things that were going on at school. He was new, and fresh, and older, and exciting.

———————

It was a strange dynamic in The Barn. Like another world. Outside of the schoolyard pecking order, away from the cliques, and the bullying, and the bullshit. Each week, Narelle's supervision would get more and more lax. In the pitch-darkness of the parish field, Mick's thin, gentle fingers crept up my shirt; his soft lips found their way to mine. Mick was funny, and easy-going, and arty, and smart. I fell for him, hard.

I started catching the crowded early bus home, getting off outside Mick's house and spending an hour or so pashing in Mick's bedroom before walking home. Mick started to call the house. I pulled at the coiled phone cord until it stretched from the kitchen all the way into the hallway. I organised to meet him in hushed tones, and covertly phoned Selina to let her know I was using her as an alibi.

'What's going on with you and Michael Callingham? He rings here a lot.' Mum endeavoured to make her inquisition seem offhand.

'We're just *friends*. God. Don't be so embarrassing.' Mum knew as well as I did that I'd never had a close friend who was a boy before, let alone a random Catholic private school vet's kid.

'I wasn't born yesterday!' Mum retorted.

'I know. You were born *ages ago*.' I stomped indignantly away to my room, outraged at her intrusion into my private life.

Word got around at school that I was dating some guy who was a year older than me, *and* a private school kid, *and* the son of a vet *and* super cute.

'Tell us about your boyfriend.' Girls from the cool cliques would turn around in the canteen line to interrogate me, but I was always tight-lipped. I didn't want to talk about Mick. I didn't want any part of what we had to be made the butt of jokes, turned into fodder for teasing. I didn't want Michael Callingham anywhere near my school. But the rumours of him still had a strangely pacifying effect. The bullying slowed down. The comments about my skin stopped as the pigment slowly returned to its usual coffee bean hue. Some cute, rich white boy saw the worth in me, and that was major playground cachet, not to be taken lightly.

'You should come and hang out at my place one day,' I said to Mick, as we polished off a box of doughnuts in the park out the back of the service station one afternoon.

'Nah.' He licked his fingers, then wiped them on my school jumper.

'Yuck! You are *so* disgusting.'

'You secretly love it.' His laughing eyes did their twinkly thing.

'No, I mean it – you should come over.' I had a deluded fantasy that once my mum met Mick properly, she wouldn't be so cautious about us hanging out together.

'Nah.'

'Why not?'

He looked at me, still chewing. 'I've seen your dad out jogging. He's built like a fucking truck!'

I threw back my head and laughed. My dad. With his meticulous record cataloguing and his nerdy building-bikes-from-scratch and his jogging-around-the-streets-in-his-daggy-headband and his scary, scary mathematics. 'Are you *serious*?' I cackled again.

'I mean it. I'm not going anywhere near your house. *Ever.*'

The youth group leader organised a minibus to take us to Mick's school musical. We wound our way through rain-slicked streets from the city's outskirts to the prestigious harbourside suburb of Milsons Point. The college grounds ran right down to the water.

The ceilings were high. Sandstone abounded. You could *feel* the history in this place. The upright Christian whiteness. Little grade seven boys with carefully parted hair stood guard at the entry doors in their grey V-neck jumpers, blue-and-yellow ties tucked in at the neck. The parents filing in – they were *something else.* All pearls and brooches and twin-sets. All roller-set hair, and diamond earrings, and that clipped faux English–accented way of speaking.

I took a seat with the dishevelled group of kids from the youth club. We'd all scrubbed up as best as we could, but we were definitely no match for this kind of poshness, though those around us smiled pleasantly enough.

And there he was. My Oberon. The most tortured king of the fairies you could ever hope to see: brown leather boots and dark eyeliner. Mick's Oberon had a carefully rehearsed *don't-sweat-it* way of delivering his lines. When Mick sang the solos, his broke-two-summers-back voice was practically Jim Morrison reincarnated. Mick's white puffy-sleeved shirt was open almost to the navel. When he smiled into the audience, I felt like he was searching for me.

For the production, Mick's school had paired with the local private girls school nearby, but I didn't notice any of the other cast members. I only saw Mick, and the way he moved across the stage. Mick, and how proud I felt that he was mine.

We milled around after the performance as the crowd filed out through the doors of the enormous hall. Mick appeared, face scrubbed clean of make-up, back in his jeans and trench coat. Running a hand through his messy longish hair, he walked over to me, slung an arm around my shoulders and turned to introduce me to the rest of the cast, who were now exiting from backstage.

'Everyone, this is Maxine.'

The girls all had long light brown hair, which hung past their shoulders, and looked as if it had just been ironed. They were wearing skinny-fit jeans with heels or slip-ons. Their jumpers were pastel-coloured and perfectly tailored. The girls stared at me, and at the random group of youth club kids standing behind me.

'*Mickey*,' one of them said. 'What a surprise!'

The girl looked me up and down, in that slow way I remembered Carlita looking at me on the first day of preschool. She *reminded me* of Carlita, or of a younger version of Carlita's mother. Her lips twitched, as if she was amused. She stepped forward, and shook my hand.

'Nice to meet you, Maxine.' There was a smirk on her lips now, as if she thought the whole situation was really funny.

I looked at Mick, who'd moved over to chat with Jed, Selina and Kurt. He hadn't noticed anything. He wouldn't. He *didn't* notice things like this, didn't *see* them. It was one of the things I liked about him, but right then, in that moment, it was frustrating.

'You coming, Mickey?' one of the girls asked, as the group made their way out of the hall.

'You're not coming back home with us?' I'd assumed Mick would catch a ride home to Kellyville with the rest of us. I wanted to sit on the back seat of the minibus, where no-one could see us, and tell him how extraordinary he'd been. I wanted to pash him till his soft sixteen-year-old stubble grazed my chin. I hated the way these girls called him *Mickey*. *Mickey* was a nickname. A *pet* name. *Mickey* sounded like a name you called someone when you knew them inside out. But, then, I only had him on weekends and the occasional weekday afternoon. I only had Mick up at The Barn. This was where he went to school, where he spent most of his time, and he was *Mickey* here.

'Nah. Closing night tonight, we're grabbing a pizza to celebrate.' He wrapped his arms around me in a quick hug, picked up his bag, and joined his friends. 'Call you tomorrow, Maxine. Thanks so much for coming to the production, guys!' He half turned, and blew a kiss in my direction.

We drifted apart after that, Mick and I, mostly through my own orchestration. I got busy with after-school activities. When he did phone, our conversations were more and more stilted. Selina was still seeing his mate Jed, and they were starting to get serious, but that was it for Mick and me. That was it for me and the first beautiful boy who made me believe that loving me was possible.

That was how it happened, or else what's a story for.

18.

EVEN THOUGH MY bedroom was the smallest in the house, it was the room I liked best. The large window faced the morning sunrise. Back when we were younger, and the room was still my father's study, us kids used to get dressed in there in the mornings, in the yellow winter light, to ward off the chill. I liked that my sister had stayed in the big double room, while I got to move into a new space, a space I hadn't seen as a bedroom before.

Three years back, when we'd been given our own rooms, Mum had thrown herself into helping us make our newly separate spaces *ours*. She'd sewn simple but elegant quilts for our beds – mine a dusty silver-grey, Cecelia's a light peach. She brought home a paint chart from the local hardware store and encouraged us to choose our own colour.

My single bed sat directly underneath the long, rectangular window. Taking up the entire length of wall opposite my bed was a darkly stained wooden sideboard-cum-bookshelf we'd found abandoned on the side of the road in perfectly good condition.

At one end of my bed was a small old-fashioned wooden desk: the straight-from-an-Enid-Blyton-book kind, with a bench seat attached, and a hinged top that you swung up and opened, to put books and pens in.

I'd always been academically inclined – or, at least, obsessed with *learning things*. Numbers had never come easily to me, nor science, but I worked hard at everything, and was always near the top of the class. Midway through high school, the inclination towards academic excellence became an obsession. It was a tangible way of proving to Greg Adams and his mates that no matter what they did, no matter what they said, no matter how hard they tried to tread me down, on paper I would always, *always* leave them in my dust.

I would get home from school, watch half an hour of television, then retire to my rose-pink bedroom and sit at the old desk, carefully attending to my homework. If an assignment didn't look right at the end, I'd start again from scratch, even if it meant staying up till eleven o'clock. At the end of every year, I stood on stage on Awards Night and cleaned up. I went in every high school musical there was, even though I was only ever cast in the chorus. I was *thirsty* for things outside of school – extracurricular activities in which kids like Greg Adams weren't involved. I was also on a conscious quest for self-worth. It didn't matter what the bullies said, I would be *better* than them. At absolutely everything. There were to be no exceptions. When I failed to get the top mark in any given subject, I grew hot with rage, admonished myself, and tripled my efforts in that area. My storybook desk was where I took care of business: my leveller. After things fizzled out with Mick, this was where I turned my attention.

The desk was disintegrating. The hinges which held the lid on were rusted and creaked when I opened the top to fish out pencils or paper. The desk was badly in need of a coat of varnish.

When I wiped it down or dusted it off, thin splinters of worn, bleached wood would come off on the kitchen sponge. But there was something about it that felt like home. I would sit on the bench seat and think about how many kids might have sat at the desk before me, in classrooms or bedrooms long gone.

I retired to my room after afternoon tea one day, and scooped my exercise books out of my schoolbag. Plonking them down on the desk, I noticed a small carefully folded rectangle of lined paper poking out from between my history and English books. Dots of red ink had bled through the paper.

Grade nine was the age of note-passing: of secrets too precious or terrifying to utter aloud. The girls in my class documented the boys they had crushes on in heart-shaped origami, which they passed around the classroom. They unfriended besties with paper aeroplanes. We wrote in our notes things bittersweet; things heartless and cruel; things hopeful and silly. Things secretive. There was a delicious, strangely Shakespearean danger about the earnest no-holds-barred confessions we poured onto the paper. There was the distinct possibility of unintended recipients – of discovery and confiscation by teachers, siblings or parents.

I sat down at my desk, casting my mind back to the day that had been. I couldn't remember either writing or receiving any notes. There was something strange about the way the note was folded: straight corner to straight corner. The creases were pressed down tightly, with the precision a nine-year-old boy might employ in the construction of a paper aeroplane. The paper was from a small, lined A5 notepad. A barely visible thin line of red wax ran across one edge, where it had been ripped from the remainder of the pad. I pulled it out from between the books, unfolded it.

Printed in large red block letters were the words: *FUCK OFF BACK TO WHERE YOU CAME FROM.*

I sat and stared at the page. Along the precision folds which had closed the piece of paper into quarters were perforated lead pencil lines which looked like they had been drawn with a ruler. Around the centre point, where the lines met in a cross, was a perfectly round lead pencil circle. The symbol looked familiar. It was only after I'd folded the piece of paper back up again that I realised it resembled a gun target – the bull's-eye view through a weapon's finder.

I walked over to my bed, lifted my mattress, and slid the piece of paper as far underneath it as I could reach. I felt alarmed, but not scared. I knew what the piece of paper was *supposed* to do, the fear it might illicit, given the right circumstances. In the movies, when people got notes like this, there were family gatherings, then community meetings. Sometimes even marches. The black people who received them were afraid. They barricaded themselves into their houses, or left town. Sometimes, if things got really out of hand, it ended in lifeless brown bodies swinging from trees.

Yet in the context of Kellyville, sitting on my silver quilt in my pastel room, staring at the moon and stars on one of my wall posters, the letter didn't fit. I wasn't *afraid*. I was sad, and angry. I was puzzled, surprised that someone hated me enough to have gone to the trouble. I was pissed off that the schoolyard had followed me home, right into my bedroom. I was furious that race hate had unfolded itself in the only space I'd been able to claim for my own.

I tried to push the letter out of my mind. The best thing to do was to try to forget about it altogether, the way I did with everything else. The school week ended. Another week or so passed, with nothing noticeably out of place. Then, in English class one morning, I set my copy of the novel I'd been reading down on the pale yellow veneer of the desk and noticed another piece of paper protruding from the pages. Same fold. Same size. Same faint dots of red on the outside, where the ink had bled through. I looked quickly around the classroom, then slid the piece of paper back between the pages of my book. I didn't want anybody to find out. I felt humiliated. I stared at the back of the teacher's pink shirt as she scrawled book review questions across the blackboard in spidery white writing. I sat with my gaze fixed to the front of the classroom wondering if *they*, whoever was writing the letters, was there in the class with me, *watching*.

When the bell went for lunch, I walked up the steps to the girls toilets, locked myself in a stall, unzipped my bag and unfolded the note. On it was a cartoon drawing of a black girl. Her lips were swollen to a ridiculous size. Her afro was tatty and minstrel-esque. The girl's broad, bulbous nose took up half of her face and was pierced with an enormous bone.

Over several weeks, the letters and drawings kept arriving. I'd find them tucked into exercise books, or my pencil case, and once even inside my lunchbox. At first they were in the same red pen and lead pencil, but as the weeks passed they became more erratic. The handwriting changed. There was one scrawled in dark green pencil; another with a hole that seemed to have been burned through the middle with a cigarette. I suspected that the stakes of the game had increased, that it was becoming a group effort.

Life continued. The banter around the dinner table at home. School debating practice. I didn't confide in anyone. If I happened to see one of the notes in the presence of anyone else, I nonchalantly covered it up. The stack of notes under my mattress grew thicker. I walked to the school bus stop a little slower. I looked in the mirror a little less. Black bruises started appearing on my skin again, after several months of being absent.

This is how it breaks us.

This is how we break.

Lockers at our high school were a privilege reserved for grade eleven and twelve students. Students in grades seven to ten wrestled with large polyester schoolbags, overprinted with the school crest. During class these bags, containing our lunch and any study materials not used in the present lesson, were lined up and left outside the classroom. I watched to see if any of my classmates took a toilet break. I buried my standard-issue school-bag among a pile of others, hoping it wouldn't be easily located. I sat towards the back of the classroom near the door to try to glimpse passers-by. I was desperate to know who was behind the letters, but resolved never to divulge the harassment to anyone. I knew what would happen. *Everyone* would find out. It would be the ultimate humiliation.

About six weeks after the first letter arrived, I opened my maths book during class and a folded piece of notepaper fluttered to the floor. Before I could retrieve it, the teacher stepped into the aisle. His fingers closed around the paper.

'Passing notes in class, Maxine?' Mr Stegall was new to the school, had started only that term. He was young – fresh out of university. The students sensed his inexperience and gave him hell.

'Can I have that back, please?' I tried to keep my voice calm.

'You certainly may not have it back. You can see me for it after class.' He tucked the note into the pocket of his pants.

My stomach seized up. Maybe he wouldn't look at the note. Perhaps he'd just give me a lecture or a detention and return it unread. I tried to think about Pythagoras' theorem, picked up my ruler to measure out a triangle. I couldn't hold my lead pencil properly. My fingers felt numb.

'What's on the note?' the girl next to me whispered.

I pretended not to hear her.

'Maxine! What's on the note?!' another girl seated behind me whispered louder, thinking I hadn't heard.

'Nothing!' I hissed back.

'Okay, girls.' Mr Stegall put down the chalk and turned to face us. 'Since everyone's so interested in this note, let's all have a read of it.'

A spot at the back of my head started to throb. My eyes followed the teacher's hand as he fished the paper out of his pocket, held it at chest level and unfolded the corners. Mr Stegall looked down at the note for a long time. He looked up at me. I lowered my eyes to the desk before they could meet his.

'You'll stay in after class,' he said quietly.

'Ooooooooooh!' The rest of the class grew rowdy.

'I bet it's porn.'

'It's a love letter.'

'As if.'

'What's it say, sir?'

'Yeah, read it out!'

'Quiet!' our teacher yelled. 'The next person to make a noise will see me at three o'clock for detention.'

The school counsellor looked most aggrieved. She remembered me well from the previous year.

'Tell me about this piece of paper, Maxine,' she said, not bothering with her standard niceties at all.

I shrugged.

'Who gave it to you?'

'I don't know.' I shrugged again, looking around the tiny windowless room.

'What do you mean you don't know?'

'I found it in my bag.'

She ran a hand over her newly cropped, bottle-red hair and stared intently at me. 'When?'

'Today. In maths class.'

'Do you know who put it there?'

'Can I go now, please?' I was supposed to be in art class. We were starting on our major work, which would account for half of our year's mark. It could be on any theme, in any media. We were supposed to be brainstorming today, and pitching our ideas to the teacher.

'Does the note bother you?'

'Not really.' I looked back at her coolly. 'I get them all the time.'

'What do you mean you get them all the time?'

I sat back in my chair and looked at her. I folded my arms over my chest. And because there was nothing else to do, I started laughing. I laughed at the shocked look on her face. I laughed at the fact that *I* was sitting in a counsellor's office because *someone else* had sent me a note peppered with slurs I encountered daily within earshot of most of my teachers.

'It's just *a little bit of teasing*,' I said, repeating the phrase she'd used last time I'd visited her office.

———————————

The school principal at my high school seemed to be constantly on rotation. At the time of the letter-writing incidents, the principal was Mr Hardy – an unkempt man in his mid-fifties whose stomach hung at least an inch over his belt. Mr Hardy was stern, and seemed constantly bothered – as if the kids whose welfare he was charged with were inconveniences, to be ignored if at all possible, and harshly disciplined if not.

'We've been trying to speak to Maxine about this and get to the bottom of it,' Mr Hardy explained to my mother, 'but we've only just found out about it, and she hasn't been very forthcoming.'

My mother stiffened in the seat next to me. 'I see,' she said, already knowing from her and my father's interrogation efforts at home that I either had no more information to give or wasn't going to reveal anything I did know.

'We're trying to *help* you,' Mr Hardy said, trying his best to sound gentle.

'Uh-huh,' I returned, rolling my eyes towards the ceiling.

On the desk in front of the principal was a clear plastic A4 sleeve filled with the notes my parents had discovered when they took my room apart.

One by one, over the course of the week, my classmates were taken out of class and questioned. When they returned to class, their eyes invariably fixed angrily on me as they took their seat in front of their Bunsen burner or laced up their sneakers for sport.

There were no letters that entire week. I was instructed to keep my bag with me at all times, but unless I was explicitly reminded to, I still left it outside. To keep the bag with me was to admit defeat. To be scared. To show that it bothered me. Still no letters. I searched for them between classes and after school. I looked frantically, right down to the lining of my backpack. I shook out every page of every book. The silence filled me with dread.

One Friday afternoon, in art class, I reached into my backpack for my sketchbook, and felt something feathery. When I lifted the book onto the table, my thick visual arts diary had been sliced clean through several times. The sketches within it had been reduced to shreds. Stunned, I handed the book over to my teacher.

Then. *Nothing.* Just like that, the letters stopped. As if they'd never been. From time to time I would see my mother visiting the principal's office after she'd dropped me off to school, but after a while, the school just seemed to stop pursuing the matter. The abuse had stopped: problem solved.

Whenever a friend passed me a note, whenever I saw a folded piece of paper, whenever the zip on my backpack was partly undone when I returned to it after a class, my stomach would flip and turn. My mind would conjure the precision-folded lined paper with the target drawn in the centre, the vile red lettering.

This is how it haunts us.

This is how it stalks.

19.

FOR MOST OF my school life, trauma manifested itself on my skin. There was a physical response that happened in the moment: the disbelief, the pins and needles deep in the pit of my stomach. The immediate fear. Afterwards, I'd descend into a steep pit of depression for an hour or so, but I'd pull myself out of it pretty quickly. I had to. There was always another class to get to; another assignment due; a bus to catch. But then the damage would show itself, flowering across my skin: the paring back of my pigment when vitiligo attacked; the thick layers of keloid scarring; the habitual skin-peeling.

I never felt completely out of control, until the incident with Bhagita Singh. Bhagita was a small lean girl. She only ever wore her beautiful long jet-black hair in a thick rope-like plait or in a ponytail with dark blue hair ties spaced evenly along it at three-centimetre intervals. Bhagita moved awkwardly. She walked on the very tips of her toes, her head and neck leading her elongated body and gangly legs around. Bhagita's school skirt hung midway to her shins, which were covered in conspicuous two-centimetre-long black hairs. Bhagita wore her light blue shirt buttoned right up to her neck. Despite her physical awkwardness, there was a surprising hardness in her piercing black eyes: a resolute confidence.

Bhagita was quiet and studious and mostly kept to herself. By grade ten, I had managed to establish a handful of friends besides Selina, but Bhagita mostly traversed the walkways linking the school buildings alone. At lunchtime, she would find a bench close to one of the staffrooms – within earshot of teacher supervision – and wolf down her lunch as quickly as possible, hunched over her green Tupperware container. Then she would walk through Chinatown, dump her bag outside on the library shelving, and spend the rest of her lunch hour working on her homework or with her nose buried in some book or other.

There was a pride about Bhagita – a sense that she truly believed she would rise above everyone around her, that she was simply biding her time. Bhagita always looked straight ahead when she walked the corridors. She never seemed to respond to any kind of taunting – didn't get visibly upset at being shunned or called names the way I did. But as far as I saw, she didn't suffer any less for this approach.

When Bhagita was being harassed, I would sink down in my seat as if trying to disappear, would covertly observe the situation out of the corner of my eye while pretending I wasn't aware of what was going on. There was never any sign at all that the taunts had penetrated Bhagita's calm. She would simply look straight ahead, shoulders square, a condescending look on her face, as if she just couldn't be bothered with the morons around her. Bhagita seemed proud, and confident, and in control – all of the things I wasn't.

Bhagita's older sister, who was two grades above us at school, was a lankier, even more uncoordinated version of Bhagita. Her name was Ghurpita, which was the cause of much schoolyard joking. Greg Adams said Bhagita and Ghurpita's dad was a *towel head*. On the days he dropped them at the front gate, pulling up directly outside the administration block in his shiny blue Mazda, you could glimpse the tight black turban wrapped from the base of his neck to his upper forehead, concealing his hair.

One multicultural day at school, Ghurpita had given the whole school a speech about being a Sikh.

'My family are members of the Sikh religion,' Ghurpita had declared boldly, and commenced a lengthy explanation of the Sikh faith, and the various different customs.

'Sikh people believe above all in the realisation of truth . . .'

Sweaty thighs had fidgeted against grubby plastic chairs. Restless, bored kids had elbowed each other and kicked at each other's feet.

'We have two prayer times every day . . .'

'Vee haff doo prayer time evelly day . . .' students around me had smirked at each other and rolled their eyes, as they altered Ghurpita's perfect unaccented English into the exaggerated mock-Indian accent they'd learned from watching *The Simpsons*.

Ghurpita's speech had gone for almost ten minutes, until even the teachers stationed at intervals around the back of the hall had started shifting from one foot to the other. I'd glanced down the rows of seats at Bhagita, who'd sat with her eyes fixed on her sister, as unfazed as ever.

There are myriad ways of telling it, but the trouble with Bhagita Singh started, once again, with my hair. This is how it happened, or else what's a story for. By the mid-nineties, migration from the African continent to Australia had increased significantly as new arrivals fled war, hunger and persecution or sought economic stability. They came from places like Sudan, Zimbabwe, Ethiopia, Zaire and Sierra Leone. Though still a tiny proportion of the Australian population, their skin colour, like mine, made them highly visible. Soon, there were enough of the new migrants that it wasn't a *total* surprise – though still very uncommon – to see another black family on the street. There would still be that nod of acknowledgement between us, but my mother didn't accost every black woman she saw and ask them over for lunch anymore.

Some of the new black arrivals had settled in affordable areas near where we lived – outer western suburbs like Parramatta, Blacktown and Mount Druitt – and in Sydney's inner west, in the not-yet-gentrified suburbs of Stanmore, Petersham and Marrickville.

Black hair salons started to spring up: Afrique Ali in King Street, Newtown, Saloon de Dreadlocks out in Fairfield. The salons were often run by African families. They offered patterned afro buzz-cuts, hair straightening, weaving, cornrowing, dread-locking and braiding: all manner of black hair management which had previously been out of reach in Sydney.

Despite the traumatic incident at Greek Charlie's a year or so before, I became fixated on the idea of having my hair micro-braided into tiny plaits. Cecelia had had it done for her birthday, so I knew it wouldn't end in disaster like the hair-straightening episode had. Cecelia's tiny braids were made up of her own hair, plus hair extensions that were individually knotted into each tiny plait at the scalp. Her hair fell way below her shoulders now, and the weight of the braids made them fall straight down and always sit in place.

The braiding had been done by a woman called Aria, from Sierra Leone. Aria imported cheap hair extensions from Africa. She'd get friends or family who were coming to Australia to pad their suitcases with the plastic packets of polyester hair. Aria worked in a bank during the week, and on the weekends she braided her customers' hair in the garage of her small, lopsided red-brick house in Petersham. She sent the extra money home to her struggling family in Sierra Leone. I saved up my pocket money for several months, until I had ninety dollars stashed in a long white envelope. My mother called Aria, and booked me in for a visit.

I sat in the cool garage and made small talk with Aria as she sectioned the long reams of hair extension and plaited them slowly into my head. Her fingers were quick – flicking this way and that, as she plaited each braid down my back. My hair has always been very thick, even for afro hair. After eight straight hours sitting in the garage, my neck began to cramp. Finally, Aria disappeared into the house, and returned with a mirror. I stared and stared at the tiny black braids hanging down my back. I looked different. I felt regal. I felt beautiful.

The first day back at school after having my hair braided at Aria's, I rounded the corner of Hectare Street to the school bus stop. A girl in my grade who lived further up our street and caught the bus from the same spot ran her hands through my minuscule plaits, letting them slowly fall back down onto my shoulders, marvelling at my new look.

'They're so pretty! Oh my god, you look just like Brandy, you look so hot. Everyone at school is going to be *so* jealous.'

'Thanks.' I bit back a triumphant smile, flicking my new long hair over my shoulder in the super casual way I'd practised in the mirror the evening before.

On the half-full early bus, it seemed as if everyone was staring at me: curiously, but somehow approvingly. With long hair, even though it was braided, I looked more *Western*. More acceptable. More like them. That morning, I walked a little taller.

The first class that day was geography. After I'd taken my seat, Bhagita Singh walked in. She sat at the desk in front of me, and set her pencil tin and notebook on the table. She turned in her seat to give my new look the once-over. I waited for her approval.

'It looks nice,' she said with a smile.

I grinned back at her. 'Thanks.'

'I liked your hair better before though.'

I was surprised by how her words stung.

'You got hair extensions?' she continued.

I glared back at Bhagita. I didn't want to talk about the process I'd gone through to make my hair sit straight, to flow down my back like hers did naturally. That would just mark me out as even weirder than I'd been before. Anyway, it wasn't her business.

'In India,' Bhagita said, as if thinking out loud, 'where my dad comes from, poor women sometimes grow their hair really long, and then they shave it off really short to sell it to Westerners. Then it's used to make wigs and stuff.'

There was no malice in Bhagita's tone, just a kind of ponderous-ness, as if she were thinking deeply about it. But in that moment, I hated Bhagita, even though I knew it wasn't human hair woven into my head, even though I knew she wasn't talking about *me*. There was something in my classmate's tone that was chastising. *Pitying.* Rage swelled inside me. This was like when my dad built me and Bronson our new bikes and then we couldn't ride them at the track because of the bullies. Like when I'd had my hair straightened and ended up with a burn. Why did Bhagita have to take this away from me – to make me feel so small for wanting hair like she already had?

'Hear that?' one of the boys whispered. 'Blackie got some dirty curry muncher's hair sewn into her head.'

'Yeah, well . . .' There was a tremor in my voice. Not an about-to-cry trembling, but a violent desperation. I closed my eyes. I could see the reddish-black veins of my inner eyelids. I felt like I wasn't in my body. Like I was watching the whole exchange unfold outside me.

'You don't have to worry about having to sell your hair, do you, Bhagita?' My voice grew louder. 'Because it stinks like curry. It's so disgusting and greasy. They wouldn't ever be able to clean it. *Nobody* would pay for your hair.'

Bhagita's eyes met mine. She held my gaze for a moment.

'I wouldn't cut my hair anyway.' She turned back around in her seat and took a biro out of her *Fantasia* pencil tin.

I suddenly recalled her sister Ghurpita's Multicultural Day Address.

'Oh. Sorry. That's right. I forgot about all that *hair is power* Sikh stuff. With the towels on the head, and the praying, and the hairy, hairy legs. From your sister Gorrillapita's *multicultural* speech.'

Selina spluttered incredulously in the seat next to me.

I didn't know what I was doing, but I knew *exactly* what I was doing. I was on autopilot, yet I knew I could stop at any time.

'Maxine's hassling the curry muncher!'

'Fucken hell, did you hear that? That was fucken *brutal!*'

I didn't have to turn to know that the voices belonged to some of my most frequent tormentors. *Maxine.* They had called me *Maxine.* Not *blackie* or *jungle bunny* or *nigger.* They had called me *Maxine.* My tormentor's voices were tinged with awe. With *respect*, if such a thing could even be possible.

This is how it entices us.

This is how we succumb.

'Quieten down, grade nine!' our teacher hissed, struggling to adjust the overhead projector so that the map of Australia became less blurry.

Bhagita had turned around to face the front of the room now. Her long coconut-oiled plait hung down in front of me, reaching right down the back of her light grey plastic chair. I unzipped my red pencil case, rummaged around and took out my purple-handled craft scissors. I slid my thumb and forefinger into the handles, held the scissors out in front of me, and snapped them loudly in the air, so Bhagita would hear the blades slicing close to her ear.

'Maybe you need a haircut,' I whispered loudly. 'Too much power,' I continued, out of earshot of the teacher. 'Too much power is never a good thing.'

This is how it grips us.

The way it draws us in.

Bhagita's shoulders tensed when she heard the scissors snapping. She shifted in her seat. I felt her fear. Bhagita was quiet for the rest of the lesson, didn't raise her hand to answer every second question like she usually did. When the bell went for second period, she quickly scooped her belongings up into her arms and was the first to leave.

That afternoon, I couldn't concentrate on studying, I sat at the desk in my room. I could hear the scissors snapping in my hands, the ugly, abusive words I'd said to Bhagita. They played over, and over, and over in my head. I felt sick about what I'd done. I wondered what Bhagita was doing; if she'd gone home and told her parents about me hassling her. I hated myself. I wanted to tear the hair extensions out of my head.

I caught the early bus to school the next morning, stashed my bag outside the library and looked for Bhagita. I spotted her down near the history reference books.

'Hi, Bhagita.'

She looked up at me from where she was balanced on her knees, browsing the shelves. She stood up and turned away from me.

'No!' I said. 'I came to talk to you about yesterday.'

Bhagita started walking away from me, *fast*.

I followed her, grabbed hold of her arm.

'Let me explain!'

'Don't touch me. Don't talk to me! GET AWAY!' Bhagita said loudly.

A hush descended over the library. Kids chatting in the glass-walled meeting rooms stared over at us. The librarian was walking in our direction. I dropped Bhagita's arm and hurried out of the library.

The look on her face was imprinted on my mind: like there was nowhere she could escape, as if I absolutely terrified her. I sat down on the wooden seats outside the library and squeezed my eyes shut. I was them. I had become *them* to Bhagita. I stood up from the bench, moved over to the flowerbeds, leaned over and threw up my breakfast.

20.

BHAGITA AND I avoided each other in the classroom. I gave her a wide berth, stayed as far away from her as possible. Eventually, she stopped flinching when I went past. Eventually, she started speaking to me again, but the guilt and shame of the episode never left me. Every time I looked at her, I saw the worst of myself.

Selina and I decided that, since the school was still taking such a lax approach to racism, we would report *everything*. Every single slight we saw in the schoolyard or in our classrooms or in the library or on the bus. We would report everything, no matter how small, whether we were involved in the incidents or not. We would take meticulous notes: of what was said, of the exact time incidents occurred, of who was involved, and who was nearby and could corroborate the account. We would stand in the principal's office every second morning and deliver our observations. We could see the grimace on his face when he saw us approaching, but there was no escape: he was duty-bound to listen.

If the bullies retaliated, or harassed us or others because of our reporting, we would walk straight back in and report them again. Eventually, a lot of the bullies got tired of being dragged out of classes; sick of the afternoon detentions; weary of their parents being dragged back up to the school again. We forced the school management to notice. We *made* them take care of business.

Throughout my high school life, I sought out the corners racism was less likely to reach: activities which relied on everyone involved coming together for a common purpose. Perhaps the thing that allowed me to channel my rage most productively was the school debating team.

The debating team comprised four students: two boys and two girls – all of them as studious as I was. We would meet in the library one lunchtime per week to brainstorm various topics and practise forming arguments. Then, every fortnight, on a Thursday afternoon, we would be excused from our respective classes and head down to the school office to borrow maroon school blazers with the school crest emblazoned on them in light blue. Another debating team would arrive at our school, or the English teacher who was our debating coach would drive us to another local high school. We would be given the topic and have about an hour to prepare our arguments.

I was the third speaker: our team's secret weapon. It was the third speaker's job to shut the argument down – to take everything the other team had said and cast doubt on it; to summarise and demolish their team's argument beyond a shadow of a doubt. I liked the position. I enjoyed drawing blood. I did it well. Our team rocketed up the debating team rankings.

There was a trick we sometimes used to exploit the judges' sympathies. It started in our school library, one debating practice. Eric, a tall, awkward, curly-haired kid who was our second speaker, discovered a book of famous quotes and speeches. Anyone who was anyone had their quotes collected in this bound volume:

John F. Kennedy, Martin Luther King, Nelson Mandela, Harriet Tubman, Abraham Lincoln.

'We should borrow this book and memorise some of the speeches so we can pull them out when we need them!' Eric said, thumbing through the thick book.

'Totally.' The other members of the team – first speaker Alicia, a petite girl with a soft, nervous voice, and our scribe Marcus, who had no interest at all in debating and really only came along to get out of class – nodded.

I borrowed the book from the library, took it home, and immersed myself in it. The speeches I memorised were mostly those delivered by black people whom I knew were held in great regard as orators: Nelson Mandela, Martin Luther King, Desmond Tutu.

The first time I used one of the speeches to sum up was against our arch nemesis team from the local selective high school: eloquent, politically astute brainiacs who were virtually unbeatable. The topic was: *That democracy is the greatest form of government.* I called the coin toss. We were allocated the negative. We knew we had no chance. It didn't matter how skilfully we presented our case, there was no way there'd be a win against democracy. Still, we went through the motions, pointing out that democracy didn't represent everyone, that it was in many ways a failed experiment: an aspiration. Then, at the end of my summing-up, I decided to quote one of Mandela's speeches.

'As Nelson Mandela stood on the docks, about to be imprisoned for more than twenty years,' I said, making sure I appeared suitably emotionally stirred, 'he looked out over his people. This is what he said. He said: "*I have cherished the ideal of a democratic and free society, in which all persons live together in harmony and with equal opportunities.*'" I could see the judges at the back of the room scribbling on their notepads. Every now and then one of them nodded approvingly. 'That great man of peace, Nelson Mandela, he said: *"It is an ideal which I hope to live for and achieve."'* I paused dramatically. '"*But if needs be, it is an ideal for which I am prepared to die.'"* I gazed into the audience of grade eights who'd been co-opted by the hosting school into attending. 'The democracy Nelson Mandela was prepared to die for *does not exist.* Not here. Not anywhere in the world. Democracy is *not* the best form of government, because *democracy* is merely an aspirational ideal.' I leaned forward. 'This great man paid a hefty price for this ultimately unachievable *idea.* How many more great men will we sacrifice?'

I returned to my seat to thunderous applause.

Eric leaned over and whispered, 'What was *that*?'

I shrugged. 'I don't know.'

'That kind of didn't even make *sense.* But they loved it!'

'That was total *evil genius*,' said Marcus, laughing.

The judges returned to the room. 'This was a tight one,' said the designated results giver. 'But in the end, though we *personally* disagreed with the negative, we felt they presented a more considered, emotional, and *heartfelt* argument.'

The other members of my debating team stared at me for a second, then we all started whooping and slapping each other on the back.

'We won!'

'Oh my god! We won! We beat them!'

We quietened down as the other team trooped over to offer their congratulations.

206

It was a trick pulled out several times over the debating season – when things weren't going well, or we were faced with a team or topic we considered unbeatable.

The topic: *That multiculturalism is Australia's greatest achievement.*

The other team called the coin toss. We were cast in the affirmative. About to deliver my final rebuttal, I glanced over at the panel of my teammates to see which speech they thought I should pull out.

'Martin Luther King,' Eric mouthed silently, shielding his lips with his cardboard prompt cards.

'Martin Luther King said, "*I have a dream*",' I boomed. 'That's what this great man said. He said, "*I have a dream that my four little children will one day not be judged by the colour of their skin*" –' I paused, as if on the verge of tears '– "*but by the content of their character.*"'

The judges nodded. The scores were tallied up. We notched another win.

I felt momentarily guilty, but I reasoned that I'd suffered so much because of racism, and here was my chance to finally get some kind of advantage out of my blackness. Besides, we weren't *technically* cheating. It wasn't my fault if we got extra points because I quoted black peaceful revolutionaries.

Our team made it to the regional finals, to be held on Australia Day at the local council chambers. Our families would be in attendance and a lot of the local politicians. We were given the topic: *That Australia Day is the greatest day for our nation.* I called the coin toss. We drew the affirmative.

Inside the preparation room, my teammates could already *feel* the win.

'This is a total no-brainer,' said Eric. 'It's *Australia Day*. I reckon the game plan should be to talk about the *terra nullius* stuff before they do. We should be like: yeah, it was genocide and everything and it was really bad, and we know there was technically an invasion on Australia Day, but Paul Keating acknowledged that, so now we all need to get over it and use it as a day to come together and celebrate in *harmony*.'

'It feels weird,' I said softly. 'That we used all of those great civil rights speeches to get here, and now we have to argue *this*.'

'It's funny,' said Eric, swinging back so his chair rocked on its back two legs. 'All of the time we were using all of those Nelson Mandela speeches, I was wondering what the judges would say if they knew that one of my ancestors was literally a slave driver.'

'What are you talking about?' I stopped scribbling notes on my notepad and stared at him.

'Well . . .' he smiled, as if it were some kind of joke. 'It's kind of true. It was my great-great-grandfather or something. He made a living driving slaves across America to be sold.' Eric's eyes met mine. He stared me down, daring me to criticise.

I swallowed hard. I sat in my chair for a few minutes, looking at the carpet while my teammates noted down their ideas on scraps of paper. I felt like we'd been in this together. But all that time – all that time – it was *me* who'd been sacrificing my integrity.

'Are you okay, Maxine?' Alicia looked over at me.

'I don't feel very well.' I took off the school blazer and frantically fanned the air in front of me with my notebook.

'Do you want me to grab a teacher?'

'No.' I gasped for air. 'I think I'll . . . I'll be okay. I can't . . . I don't feel well though . . . Marcus will have to speak instead of me. I'll go scribe this time.'

'Marcus has never spoken before. He's never debated before.'

'He'll have to. That's what the extra team member is supposed to be for anyway. I feel really sick.'

'We're going to lose if you don't go third.' Alicia looked at me, indignant tears brimming in her eyes.

'Well, he'll have to this time. I don't feel well.' I got up from the table and exited the preparation room. I made my way outside into the council chamber grounds and stood next to the sausage sizzle stand, breathing in the summer air. Along the council chamber lawns, royal blue Australian flags fluttered in the summer breeze.

The public speaking and debating circuit was another world. Here, you could also be bullied and beaten, but you lived and died not by brute force, but by word. Everyone was supposedly considered equal, it was a level playing field, and that notion still appealed to me. After I left the debating team, I found myself on the school public speaking circuit.

The school nominated me as their entrant for the Lions Club Youth of the Year competition. There were to be two categories: a current affairs quiz, and a public speaking element in which entrants could choose a topic of their choice and speak for seven minutes.

The current affairs interviews took place at the home of one of the Lions Club board members. We pulled up outside, my mother and I, in our second-hand Nimbus.

'Should I come in with you?' Mum rested her hands on the steering wheel.

'Nah. I reckon it'll be fine.' I checked the clock on the dashboard, peered past the flowering gardenias and musk trees on the front lawn of the double-storey home. A boy around my age was coming out of the front door in his maroon school blazer. He stopped on the doorstep and loosened his tie before heading off down the street.

The screen door opened before I touched it. A woman in her mid-sixties ushered me into a small lounge room, gesturing towards a floral couch.

'Maxine Clarke?' she checked.

I nodded.

'Pleased to meet you, Maxine. I'm Susan.' She held out her hand and introduced herself, then pointed to a grey-haired man seated in a nearby armchair and introduced him as well. The man sat up in his seat, looking over at me with interest.

'Frank and I will be asking you a few current affairs questions this afternoon, before your public speaking event at the club tonight.'

'Hello, Maxine.' The man looked down at the A4 pad balanced on his lap. 'It's great to meet you. Why don't you tell us a little bit about yourself?'

'Um . . . I'm in grade ten. I'm doing this competition because I really love public speaking,' I lied, smiling. 'I used to be on the debating team, but I quit to concentrate a bit more on my studies going into grade eleven. I'm so glad to have been nominated for this competition, though.'

Public speaking wasn't nearly as attractive a proposition as debating had been. There was no direct kill in it, even if you won, and there was no bare-knuckled word-tussling to be had. But I hadn't been able to get out of the Youth of the Year competition; my English teacher had begged me to enter, and I'd been given a lot of time off my normal lessons in order to prepare.

210

'Where are you from, Maxine?'

For fuck's sake. I kept the smile pasted on my face. 'I was born in Sydney, and grew up in Kellyville,' I said cheerily.

The woman smiled, as if mildly amused that I didn't understand what old Frank was getting at.

'Where were your parents born, I mean, sweetheart?' asked Frank. 'You're a very *striking* young woman.' Frank was leaning forward, a patronising smile on his face.

'*Frank!*' the woman scolded.

'What?' Frank looked annoyed. 'She's a lovely young lady, Susie.' He turned back to me. 'What part of the world did you say they were from?'

'My dad was born in Jamaica, my mum's from Guyana,' I said, curtly but politely.

'Your mum's from Ghana? I have an old friend who lived there for a while.' Frank wrote something down on his notepad.

'No, she's from *Guyana*,' I corrected him.

'You must mean *Ghana*.' Frank shook his head, smiling.

'*Guyana*, in the West Indies,' I said.

'You have those striking African looks!' he responded. 'I very much doubt your mum's from India.' He and Susan chuckled.

'Now,' said Susan, checking her watch and adjusting her gold-rimmed spectacles, 'we should get started on these current affairs questions – the next contestant will be here in fifteen minutes!'

I closed my eyes for a second longer than a blink; beat back my anger.

———

The Lions Club hall was decked out for dinner festivities. Long tables were covered in bleached white cotton tablecloths; small bouquets of flowers sat in the centre of each. Dad had a late lecture that he wasn't able to get out of, but Mum had forced Cecelia and Bronson to tag along. Their sullen faces made no attempt to hide their lack of interest.

Youth of the Year contestants slowly filed into the room, accompanied by their families. The rest of the audience was older – dressed in suits and ties, or calf-length skirts and prim blouses. Most of the other contestants looked familiar from my time spent on the debating circuit. As they arrived, I slowly weighed each of them up. Anthony Hawkins, from Model Farms High School. He spoke too slowly and too softly; he had no fire in him. Lucinda Morgan, from Baulkham Hills Selective High School. It was weird that Baulko had selected her to represent them. She was smart, but she gestured wildly when she got excited and had this strange way of turning up the end of every sentence, like she was posing a question. It worked in a debate, if she wasn't the last speaker, but it wasn't ideal for a speech. John Calvin, from Castle Hill High School. I smiled to myself. Not a chance.

A thin girl with a small silver nose-ring entered the room, wearing a uniform I couldn't immediately place. Her dyed-black hair was cropped short and feathered around her ears. She wore dark eyeliner and was all pared-back goth. She stared around the room, glowering. The tall man next to her wore a beautifully tailored black jacket with a crisp white shirt and blue JAG jeans. The moment they entered the room, I knew her dad was *somebody*. The Lions Club members turned to smile at the twosome, and crane their necks. Several people got up and edged their way around the tables to shake the man's hand. He put his hand on the girl's shoulder.

They sat near the back of the room. The girl slid a series of palm cards out of her skirt pocket, shuffled them nervously. She was an unknown for sure. A wildcard. I wondered what her story was.

There are many ways I could tell it. The truth is, I can't now recall what any of the speeches were about, even my own. I only remember the girl's nervousness; the way her voice trembled when she spoke; the way her eyes darted quickly around the room the few times she actually looked up from her palm cards. It sounded as if she had never done any public speaking before. Her words were stilted.

There was a look of shock and embarrassment on her face when they called her name as the winner of the public speaking section. I turned in my chair to look at her father. The man sitting next to him slapped him on the back in congratulations, but the goth girl's dad didn't respond. He stared directly back at me. Our eyes locked. His expression was unreadable.

'Well, I guess that's that then,' Mum said, as the waiters moved in to clear the half-eaten plates of watery panna cotta.

We rose from our seats as the audience began to make their way out of the hall.

'Excuse me.'

There was a hand on my arm. I looked up, surprised. The girl with the nose-ring was standing behind me with her dad.

'Hi,' she said, her certificate still in one hand.

'Hi. Congratulations,' I said. 'You were good.'

She looked as if she was about to cry.

'You don't have to say that,' her dad said, his face flushed pink with embarrassment. 'You were excellent.' He was looking me right in the face. I could sense the people around us slowing, leaning in to listen.

'Thanks.' I shrugged, and pushed my chair in under the table.

'No,' he said emphatically. 'You were *excellent*.' He reached over and held out his hand to my mother, who shook it firmly. 'Tell your daughter she was incredible.'

'Thank you,' Mum said.

'You keep doing this,' the man said, shaking a finger at me. 'You were the best speaker here.' Then the two of them turned and made their way through the throng of well-wishers towards the photographer waiting at the other end of the hall to do a photo shoot for the local paper.

This is how we shame it.

How we make it break.

21.

AS WE MOVED towards senior high school, student numbers began to dwindle. Kids who weren't academically inclined joined the trade stream and were funnelled out into various local TAFE programs. Some were offered full-time jobs at Pizza Hut or the local car mechanic's or Coles. School became much more bearable.

Sometimes, Eric, Marcus and Alicia from the debating team or a handful of other interchangeable friends would sit on the lawn with Selina and me at lunchtime. We had a loose friendship group now, of sorts. We'd skylark around, talking about nothing in particular, as we lay on our backs, soaking up the sunshine.

Marcus from debating happened much the same way Mick had a year earlier. All of a sudden, we just *were*, he and I. This is how it happened. This is what a story's for. Marcus had long, wavy brown hair that fell down past his shoulders. He was slim, and fidgety, and still had braces on his teeth. Marcus was a grunger. He played the electric guitar; listened endlessly to The Doors and Deep Purple on his silver Sony discman. He had the eyes of a young Paul McCartney: warm, brown, earnest and drooping downwards a little at the outside edges.

I wasn't sure *exactly* how much I liked him. But he was funny, and nice, and he really liked *me*, and that seemed good enough. Marcus was different from Mick. Marcus went to my school. He knew what the deal was. He liked me, and he didn't care who knew it. He liked me, and he didn't give a flying fuck what anyone thought. That was worth a lot.

We went to Skate 2000, a local roller rink. We held hands as we skated around in the strobe-lit darkness to Kylie Minogue and Roxette, whose music we both hated, falling over each other and our own feet. We sat by the radio at my place making obscure mix-tapes: alternating my R&B taste with his grunge rock.

———————

I was sitting on the polished floorboards of our hallway one summer afternoon chatting to Marcus, the telephone cord stretched as far as possible from my mum, who was pottering around in the kitchen.

'What are you up to?'

'Nothing much. It's bloody hot.'

'I know.' Marcus was eating Cheezels on the other end of the line.

'Will you *stop* crunching those in my ear!'

'Okay, okay. *Jeez.*' I could hear him setting the chip packet aside. 'I'm going to get off the line now anyway. I'm going for a swim.'

'Rub it in, why don't you?'

Marcus had an in-ground pool in his backyard. I could hear Mum behind me, the creak of the dishwasher door opening just behind the hallway wall as she found an excuse to linger near my end of the conversation.

'You should come over for a swim,' Marcus suggested. 'Get your mum to drop you over.'

I paused. I'd never been to Marcus's house before, though he'd been to mine a handful of times. With Mick, it had been different. Mick's dad was always in the vet practice below the house. He'd just wave if he saw me walking past the window. Mum barely knew I was hanging out there, but Mick's parents were pretty relaxed. And they knew our family. There was no *Look Who's Coming to Dinner* situation: nervous black partner enters white-picket-fenced home in the suburbs. I had no reason to believe Marcus's family would have an issue with the two of us, based on what I knew about them, but I wasn't sure I wanted to put myself through the stress of finding out.

This is how we edit our lives.

How we brace against the blows.

'Go on, ask your mum!'

The air conditioners at either end of our house were on full pelt, but they didn't seem to be making a dent in the heat. I ran my finger down the wall in front of me. 'Now?'

'Yeah. Come over.'

'Hang on. Let me ask.'

I scooted across the floor on my bottom and poked my head around the corner and into the kitchen. 'Can I go over to Marcus's house for a swim?'

'Today?' Mum lifted a handful of clean cutlery out of the dishwasher and dumped it into the drawer.

'Yeah. He just invited me. Can I go? *Please?* It's bloody hot.'

'Mind your language. Are his parents home?'

Maxine Beneba Clarke

'*Mum!*'

'Well?'

'*Yes,*' I said indignantly. 'His mum's home.'

'Let me talk to her.' Mum held her hand out for the receiver.

'My mum wants to talk to your mum,' I groaned into the receiver.

'Muuuuuum!' Marcus yelled.

'Jesus. Did you have to yell that *into* the receiver?' I handed the phone over to Mum, and stood in the kitchen watching her.

'Hi, it's Cleopatra here, Maxine's mum.' She paused. 'Hi, Peta. Oh, have you?' She raised an eyebrow at me, then turned her back towards me. 'Yes, I believe he did.' Another pause. 'Okay. Okay. Yes, that sounds great. Thanks, Peta, let me just write the address down. Okay. Yep. Looking forward to meeting you.' Mum handed the phone back to me, and continued unloading the dishwasher.

'So can you come over now?' Marcus asked.

'Yeah. Yeah, I guess I'm coming over!'

———————

Their house was small: cottage-like. A flower-rimmed path led up to the pine front door.

'Looks nice.' Mum switched off the engine.

The front door opened. Marcus and his mother walked over to the car. I leaped out the passenger-side door as Marcus's mum leaned into the driver's window to talk to Mum.

I followed Marcus through the front hallway, past the kitchen and up a small flight of stairs to his room. An acoustic and an electric guitar were propped up in the corner near a CD player and a music stand.

'You want to swim first or hang out a bit?' He looked at my duffel bag.

'Let's swim. Where's the bathroom? I'll get changed.'

The bathroom was all white and beige, and impossibly clean, like in one of those display homes. As if no-one ever used it. I pulled my swimmers on, then put a t-shirt over the top, adjusting the short sleeves to make sure my chicken pox scars were covered. I looked in the bathroom mirror, and took a deep breath in. When the shirt got wet and clung to my body, Marcus would notice the scars, and probably his mum would too. I thought about *Chinese straight*: the visit to Greek Charlie's salon; the pool party from several years back. I wrapped my towel around my waist and walked back to Marcus's room.

Splashing around in the pool, screaming *Marco Polo* at each other, I forgot about everything. The scars. My self-consciousness. We played around in the water until Marcus's mum called us in for food.

Marcus's dad and brother were back from his brother's football game. His mum introduced us and we made small talk as she set a teacake and some fruit on the table.

Marcus's dad had the same puppy dog eyes as his son, only older and less mischievous. 'Marcus says you're pretty into public speaking,' he said casually.

'Yeah.' I looked over at Marcus, who shrugged back at me.

'You know —' his dad scratched his closely trimmed grey-flecked beard, '— my boss at work, she *met* Dr Martin Luther King. Years ago, of course, when he was alive. She heard him speak, in the States. *In the flesh.*' He looked at me pointedly.

I took a bite of my apple, so I didn't have to speak immediately. The man was just trying to be nice, I knew it. Silence unwound itself across the table as he waited for some sign of approval.

'Oh,' I said, trying to signal somehow that my interest was purely rhetorical. I was a little intrigued. I wanted to know what the circumstances were – how this woman had come to be in Dr King's presence. Whether she was at a civil rights rally where he'd just happened to be speaking or had known him on a work or personal level. I didn't want to ask, though. I didn't want my boyfriend's dad thinking that the best way to interact with me was to start a conversation about civil rights in the deep American South. But the man was trying so hard to be nice – trying to make me feel welcome in his home. I didn't want to be disrespectful either. The back of my head started to throb, in the spot that always ached when this kind of interaction happened. Marcus's dad looked disappointed by my apparent lack of interest.

There were many more visits to Marcus's house. Swims, and movie dates, and jam sessions. His parents went out of their way to make me feel welcome, but there was always something, always some comment or other that was slightly out of place.

'I like your hair,' his mother said to me approvingly one day as I headed past her to the swimming pool. 'Those kind of braids are called *cornrow braids*, aren't they?'

'They are.'

She must have sensed the surprise in my voice. 'I learned that from watching *Oprah* the other day,' she confessed, smiling.

They were genuinely interested in me, Marcus's parents, but it felt as though I was some fascinating exotic thing that had entered their lives; a conversation starter. Sometimes I felt awful for thinking that, and tried to convince myself it was all in my head, that I was just being paranoid. At other times, my interaction with Marcus's family seemed to confirm my worst fears.

There was a kids' clothing catalogue sitting folded on the kitchen counter one afternoon. The model on the front was about two years old, with dark honey-coloured skin and curly black hair.

'Mixed-race babies are so adorable,' Marcus's mum gushed. Then her hand fluttered up towards her mouth. 'You do say *mixed race*, don't you? I mean, you wouldn't say *half-caste* anymore, would you?'

I bristled. 'No,' I said. 'You definitely wouldn't.'

At school, Marcus and I became established as an item. Sometimes he'd walk the corridors with his arm slung loosely around my shoulders. For several terms, we became one of those schoolyard couples, almost always seen together.

But my second teenage relationship was destined to be just as short-lived as the first. The Biscuit Fiasco. *That* was the beginning of the end. That West Indian way of singing a tale; this is how it riffed.

One lunchtime, we were sitting on the small grassy mounds out behind the English classrooms: Selina, Alicia, Eric, Marcus and me. Marcus took a foil-wrapped package out of his bright yellow lunchbox, unwrapped a small pile of biscuit treats and started eating. I stared, mesmerised, at the biscuit journeying from his hand to his mouth and back again.

'Is that . . . ?' Selina elbowed me, whispering softly.

She and I exchanged glances. 'It is.'

'What the fuck are you eating, Marcus?' I asked loudly.

'Biscuits?!' he said, giving me a quizzical look. 'Want one?' My boyfriend held the packet out to me.

The chocolate biscuit stared up at me, its shock of hair haloed out around its face. A cute little button-up jacket and a little pair of slacks were indented onto its torso and legs. Its familiar wide golliwog eyes stared into mine. It grinned at me, as if to say: *Come on, I'm delicious.*

'I'm not eating a fucking Golliwog biscuit, Marcus.'

Selina and Eric laughed. Marcus looked genuinely confused.

'They're *racist!*' Selina exclaimed, shocked at his lack of shame. 'They're *offensive!*'

'Oh, *that.*' He bit into another biscuit. 'They're not even *called* Golliwog biscuits anymore. They changed the name, like, a couple of years ago. They're called *Scallywags* now.'

'They're still fucked,' I said quietly.

'Calm down!' Marcus laughed. Brown crumbs of Golliwog biscuit were caught along the front wires of his braces. He reached out and took a swig of water from his drink bottle.

Because he was my boyfriend; because he and his family were always so lovely to me; because he was nice, and good-natured, and meant no harm, I forgave him. But sometimes I would look over at Marcus in class, or when we were playing Marco Polo at his house, and in my mind, I'd see those chocolate Golliwog crumbs caught in the metal wires.

Several weeks later, Marcus's hand was threaded through mine as we walked back to his house after school one Friday afternoon. He picked up our intertwined hands and inspected them.

'I like the way our hands look, together like this,' he said.

'What do you think this is?' I retorted cynically, 'A "Heal the World" video?'

'Ouch. You're *harsh!*' he chastised me. 'No, I mean, I just . . . I like your hand. The way the brown on the back of your hand

222

meets the white of your palm, on the edge there. It looks . . . cute. Like a paw or something. Like a possum paw.'

It was there, all of a sudden, out of nowhere. Walking home with my boyfriend, when I least expected it. The dry tongue. The nakedness. That can't-think freeze.

'What . . . what did you say?'

'I didn't mean . . . I just meant . . .'

I unwound my fingers from his and took a step away from him on the footpath.

I was Patch again. Seven years old, standing in the line for tunnel ball. *You look like my dog. He's got white and brown patches all over him too. Fetch, Patch! Go fetch, doggy!*

We continued walking towards Marcus's house in silence.

Greg Adams was there with us, walking between me and my boyfriend. Lachlan Jones was there too, pushing his face close to mine. *We can't put you on my Fuck Chart, Maxine. Sorry, but animals don't count.*

'I'm sorry.' Marcus looked mortified at his mistake. 'I really didn't mean anything by it.'

'Don't worry about it. Nah, it's fine. I'm fine.'

We walked on towards his house, side by side. You could have cut the air between us with a knife.

I moved through the afternoon at Marcus's as if under water. Everything seemed distant; blurred. I made polite conversation with his mum, waited out the two hours or so until my mum swung by to pick me up. I didn't want things to end like they had with Mick. I didn't want to just give up because it got too hard. Because I'd overreacted to something. But every time I thought about hanging out with Marcus, I remembered the chocolate biscuit crumbs in his braces; the animal he'd likened me to. Marcus, for his part, kept trying. He seemed confused by the growing distance between us.

There were things that couldn't be unsaid or unheard.

There were thoughts he'd had that he couldn't take back.

This is how it happened.

This is how it happened, or else what's a story for.

22.

FOR THE FIRST time, in the mid-nineties, I was thoroughly aware of a shift in public and political sentiment around multiculturalism and immigration. I'd started to browse the weekend papers every now and then. The letters sections contained angry comments about Aboriginal people, about Asians, about migrants like my parents.

There was a red-haired woman – a politician. Pauline Hanson, her name was. Pauline used to run a fish-and-chip shop in Ipswich in south-east Queensland, and spoke with a nasal country twang. Pauline Hanson said Asians were coming to Australia and forming ghettos, that this was *her* land, and she should get a say in who came into the country, just like she had a say in who entered her house. Pauline Hanson said multiculturalism was the real problem with Australia and should be abolished immediately.

We watched on the news as Labor Prime Minister Paul Keating lost the 1996 election to John Howard, one of the Liberal Party's most dyed-in-the-wool conservatives. Along with the new Liberal government came Pauline Hanson, elected to the House of Representatives as an independent. Pauline's maiden speech

sounded much like the Rivers of Blood address Enoch Powell
had delivered in England in 1968 . . . *in fifteen or twenty years'
time, the black man will have the whip hand over the white man . . . We
must be mad, literally mad, as a nation.* Her views started circulating
more widely in the media, gaining traction. We watched from
the lounge room of the house on Hectare Street as xenophobia
slowly ate up more broadcast time. Pauline Hanson terrified me.
She sounded like Greg Adams at my school: only grown up,
a little more tactful, and with a much broader reach.

There was one day of the year at my high school when being
black was celebrated, at least by the teaching staff: Multicultural
Day. On Multicultural Day, students came to school in multicultural mufti dress. Those few students who came from migrant
or diverse backgrounds would wear the traditional dress of their
homeland – a sari, say, or a Polish folk costume. The rest of the
students would wear their ordinary weekend clothes with some
token 'multicultural' item: chopsticks through a hairbun, a brightly
coloured 'Jamaican rasta' wig complete with felt dreadlocks, or a
stick-on bindi in the centre of their forehead. Inside the classroom,
within earshot of the teachers, proceedings were as civilised as
a junior United Nations. Outside in the playground, those in
'traditional' dress would be mercilessly bullied.

The central focus of Multicultural Day was the assembly, at
which a handful of students were trotted out to spruik their wares.

This is how it happened, how the melody played. Gasps and
guffaws in all the right places. That folklore way, of singing a
tale. At the start of grade eleven, as Multicultural Day approached,
the head of the English and Drama faculty made his way towards

where Selina and I lay sprawled on the grass behind the English block, basking in the lunchtime sun.

'Afternoon, girls,' he said in his customary dour tone.

Selina and I stopped our chatting, looked at him curiously.

'Hi,' we responded in unison.

Mr Brady cleared his throat. 'Miss Silverstein tells me you're studying, um, belly-dancing . . . Selina.' Mr Brady cleared his throat. Do you think you could . . . would you like to give a performance at the Multicultural Day assembly?'

I'd seen Selina dance. It was incredible – she was all feet-sharply-stamping and hips swaying at spellbindingly graceful angles.

'Okay,' Selina said, her cheeks flushing a medium pink.

I glanced at her in surprise.

'You're happy to do that?' Mr Brady double-checked.

'I think so.'

'Great. I'll ask your drama teacher if you can have a few lessons off to rehearse, and then perhaps you can show us what you're going to do before you perform.'

Selina and I looked at each other, both aware that if Selina was *out of class* rehearsing, I would be *in the class*, on my own.

'Do you want me to do something as well, sir?' I asked hope-fully. The previous year, on account of my debating experience, my English teacher had asked me to give a speech at the assembly. I'd spoken about activism – about Rosa Parks and the Montgomery bus boycotts. I'd regurgitated the Martin Luther King and Nelson Mandela speeches I still had memorised and talked about the way in which their anti-racist activism had made such a difference to so many. It was some small penance, in my mind, for having exploited their speeches throughout the debating season.

I'd given the speech knowing it would be the basis for harass-ment outside the assembly hall. I figured it would be no worse than the teasing I usually encountered, and had felt strangely triumphant that my tormentors would first have to listen to me preach tolerance for five minutes.

Sure enough, the speech had provided them with weeks of ammunition.

'Here comes Rosa. Let's vacate her seat up the back of the bus!' someone on the bus had yelled out, to roars of laughter, as I boarded.

'I have a dream,' some kid would declare dramatically as they passed by where I sat eating my chicken-and-lettuce sandwich at lunchtime. 'I have a dream that I will never have to listen to one of blackie's stupid boring speeches again.'

'Well . . .' Mr Brady said, 'we were thinking this year we would make the assembly a little more . . . *entertaining.*' He paused for a moment. 'Do you do any kind of . . . *cultural dancing*?'

I squinted at him. His thick form was silhouetted against the sun. 'I can do a cultural dance if you want me to.'

Mr Brady looked me square in the eyes. 'Have you taken dancing lessons?' he asked.

'Yes,' I replied, recalling the disastrous term Cecelia and I had spent sashaying to 'Walk Like an Egyptian' at Debbie's Dynamic Dance Academy. The lyrics started bopping in my head. Words about men gathered by the Nile smoking hookah pipes, about all the 'foreign types' doing the sand dance. I waited for the teacher to respond.

'What kind of dance are you studying?' Mr Brady looked very interested now. 'It would need to be *cultural.* Like some kind of tribal dancing or something?'

'I can do tribal dancing,' I said emphatically. Out of the corner of my eye I could see Selina staring at me incredulously.

'This is going to be great, girls!' Mr Brady enthused. 'I'll talk to your drama teacher about having you both released from class next week to rehearse.' He turned and headed back towards the faculty building.

'I didn't know you were doing dancing classes,' Selina said curiously.

'You don't know *everything* about me,' I said, deliberately avoiding meeting her gaze.

Selina looked shocked. I knew she was probably remembering the racist letters I'd kept from her for so long and thinking maybe I was right.

'I do a dancing class in Parramatta. On the weekends.'

'Oh. Okay.' Selina ran her hand uncertainly through her long, dark ponytail, tugging out the knots with her fingers as she stared back at me.

I was already regretting my dishonesty. I was sure my lie would eventually get me into a whole shitload of trouble, and I didn't want my friend to be embroiled in it. But until the teachers found out, we'd get to hang out together away from everyone else. It was totally worth it.

For the next week, we were excused from drama classes. We'd head to an empty classroom, where we'd kick our shoes off, lie on the floor and eat potato crisps while we gossiped and flicked through *Smash Hits* magazines.

We'd play Selina's belly-dancing music loudly on the CD player we'd borrowed from the faculty staffroom, keeping one eye on the door and one eye on the window, leaping to our feet to do 'dancing stretches' any time the shadow of a teacher or student passed by.

When I stopped to think about it, I felt consumed with guilt about lying to Selina and to my drama teacher. The fiery-haired, cheerful Miss Silverstein was one of the good ones: vigilant, passionate, encouraging, in that way younger un-daggy teachers can be with the more studious and enthusiastic of their charges.

At the end of the week, Miss Silverstein suddenly appeared at the door as the bell went for the end of the lesson. 'Mr Brady and I were thinking that you could show us your dances tomorrow at lunchtime, girls, since the assembly's on Monday,' she suggested. 'So please make sure you bring your music and costumes to school tomorrow, and anything else you might need.' She left the room.

My mouth went dry. Selina looked at me. I forced myself to smile confidently. I hadn't really thought ahead to how I was going to claw my way up out of the very deep hole I'd dug for myself. I could try to feign sickness tomorrow and on Monday, but I was pretty sure my mother wouldn't buy it. I could say I'd suddenly got stage fright, but given my central role in the school band, the debating team and pretty much any performance that was going, no-one would believe me. My stomach turned flips.

The nausea stayed with me throughout the day. On the late bus home, as the white-picket-fence, dog-cat-four-wheel-drive-and-pool suburbia of Baulkham Hills fell away outside the window, my regret slowly turned into anger.

I was angry that the school did little to combat the insidious racism I dealt with on a daily basis, but was happy to watch me utilise my blackness to win them a debating championship, or parade me and the rest of their 'multicultural contingent' around when the circumstances suited. I was angry that my speech the previous year about anti-racist activism had apparently either ruffled so many feathers or been of so little interest that *cultural dancing* was now the organising committee's preference. *Fuck it.* I pressed my forehead against the cold, grimy bus window. *If Mr Brady wants cultural dancing, I'll give him cultural dancing.* Cecelia was at university now anyway. There was no-one to dob me in, so I had a good chance of getting away with it.

When I arrived home, I went straight to the laundry and dug my mother's jazzercise leotard out of the washing basket. The leotard was a shimmering bronze bodysuit. Around the bust and stomach, the lycra had faded to a dull brown. Any time we saw Mum heading out to class wearing it, Cecelia, Bronson and I took a twisted pleasure in ribbing her about the indecency and innate *wrongness* of a brown person wearing a same-as–skin-tone leotard out in public.

In my bedroom, I paired the leotard with an earth-toned skirt. The cheesecloth skirt was one of my summer favourites: it had once been flowing and ankle-length, but I'd recently cut it off just above the knee. The unhemmed edge had unravelled into a two-inch-long fray all the way around. Staring into the full length mirror that leaned against my bedroom wall, I plaited my long braids into one fat plait, then wound it up into a knot on the top of my head. I grabbed my four wooden bead necklaces from where they hung on my bedpost and wound one around each ankle and one around each wrist. The costume didn't look all that authentic, but it was going to have to do. I undressed quickly, and hurriedly put my school uniform back on before anyone could barge in and spring me in my costume.

There was only one CD of African music in my collection. I shoved it into my CD player and scrolled through the album, listening to the openings of each song. In the relative privacy of my bedroom I twisted this way and that, trying to come up with some distinctly African-flavoured moves.

———————

At lunchtime the next day, Selina and I took our dancing costumes into the English department toilet block and disappeared into the cubicles to get ready. As I emerged from the toilet stall, Selina shot me a strange look, but she didn't comment. Inside the drama classroom, after Selina had demonstrated her belly-dancing, I slipped my African CD into the CD player, and jiggled and jumped around the room with my face set in a serious expression. I clasped my hands together, squatted and jumped with both knees pointed outwards. I twirled around with one hand raised high above my head, as if worshipping the heavens. I got down on my knees, and thumped passionately on the ground.

'That was fantastic, girls!' said Mr Brady. 'Thank you so much for agreeing to share your cultural experience with the rest of the school. I'm sure the other kids will really appreciate it.'

I stared back at him and Miss Silverstein in disbelief.

———————

On Multicultural Day, I hid behind the black curtain of the stage in the school auditorium, watching Selina glide across the stage in front of the bemused student mass. Her hair fell almost to her waist. She was dressed in a deep purple skirt and red bra top. Bells jangled across her hips. The rest of the kids seemed stunned. Some clapped loudly. Others turned to the person next to them open-mouthed, as if to verify what they'd just seen. Selina exited the stage from the other side. My music started playing. I ran onto the stage, trying not to look at the audience as I shook, jumped, stamped and wiggled to the music. I ran quickly off the stage. The audience applauded us heartily.

Backstage, one of the other drama teachers, Mr Payne, was handling the exits and entrances for the special assembly.

'Wow, that was incredible,' he said. 'My grade twelves are studying Greek drama at the moment for their HSC unit. We've been talking about how Greek choruses used to dance really expressively to show emotion and advance the storyline.'

I nodded impatiently, unsure where the conversation was going and uncomfortable about standing around in my cobbled-together costume.

'I reckon your dancing might be similar to what a Greek chorus would do. Do you know other tribal dances that have different meanings or stories behind them? Would you be happy to come and perform a few of them for us in class next week? I can speak to your teachers about you having some time off class.'

'Sure.' I looked back at him expressionlessly, fatigued by the charade.

At home, over the weekend, I listened to my African album again and came up with two other rough dances, and duly presented myself at Mr Payne's classroom the following week.

Apart from a handful of grade twelve boys tittering behind their hands, Mr Payne's class was serious and attentive. After my performance, there was a question time for the students.

'How long have you been learning?'

'Two years,' I said, a little too emphatically, shifting my weight from foot to foot.

'Whereabouts in Africa are the dances from?'

'Uh . . . West Africa?' It came out like a question, rather than a definitive answer.

'Does your whole family do tribal dancing?'

I broke into an involuntary smirk. I started laughing, imagining my mother, sister, dad and brother joining me on stage, each of us wearing makeshift fake costumes and stamping about. Once the image took hold, I couldn't dispel it. 'No!' I kept cackling loudly – couldn't stop. After a few seconds, I managed to pull myself together. 'This is something that only I do. By myself. On my own. It's my *special thing*.'

Mr Payne stared at me intently. 'I think that'll do for today,' he said curtly. 'Thanks for coming and sharing that with us, Maxine.'

———————————

Over the next few weeks, I waited for the lies to catch up with me, but no-one at school ever pulled me up about my tribal dancing ruse. Oddly enough, I was bullied much less for my tribal dancing display than I was for my general existence – in the playground, the whole cultural display barely rated a mention.

About a month after my performance for Mr Payne's grade twelve class, I arrived home from school, dumped my bag in the hallway, walked to the fridge and noticed Mum sitting at the kitchen table, watching me.

'Hi, Maxine,' she said, with a strange tone in her voice.

'Hi, Mum.' I dug a cold pear out of the fruit bin.

'I was over at Mary Smith's house today,' she said.

'Oh,' I said, biting into the pear. 'How is she? What's new?' Mary Smith was a large, loud but good-natured woman who was Kellyville's premier gossip. Anything you wanted to know about anyone in the village, she was somehow good for – and would usually offer up the bulk of her information before anyone even cared to ask.

'Her daughter Jane is doing HSC drama. In Mr Payne's class.'

The bit of pear suddenly caught in my throat.

'She said to tell you that Jane really enjoyed the tribal dancing you did for her class.'

My hands suddenly felt clammy. I slowly pushed the fridge door shut, considered my options. 'Oh, that's nice,' I said in a calm, measured voice, turning to look at Mum. 'I'm so glad everyone at school had their lives so deeply enriched by my *cultural display*.'

Mum stared at me for a moment, an incredulous look on her face. The corner of her mouth twitched slightly as I turned and went down the hallway to my room. The incident was never raised again in our household, but my tribal dancing career had come to a very definitive end.

23.

WHEN I FIRST heard I was going to get braces, I was ecstatic. I told everyone at school – anyone who'd listen. Braces were *distinctive*. They were unusual and temporary, like wearing a plaster cast on your leg. You could accessorise the little rubber bands that joined the braces together, matching the colours with your plastic bangles or fluoro hair scrunchies. I didn't even care that I'd have to take a hiatus from my position as lead trumpeter in our school band. Wearing braces was something *normal* kids did. Maybe I would even be called *metalmouth*, like some of the other kids at school who had braces. It would be a welcome distraction from the ordinary taunts.

Wearing braces turned out to be painful business. Each fortnight, Cecelia and I would go to the orthodontist to have them tightened, and for the next few days, the bones in our jaws would ache. I could feel the pull right down to the centre of my skull.

After eighteen months, our mouths came good. I looked similar to how I had always looked, only with my out-of-line eye tooth pulled back into the row, but my sister had somehow changed. It was more than just losing her overbite. While Cecelia's teeth were being straightened, the rest of her bones had sorted themselves out as well. Her cheekbones were now more pronounced. Her legs, which had been long and gangly, were lean and toned, with just the right amount of muscle. Her haughtiness had somehow transformed into poise. There was something exquisitely and effortlessly aloof about the way my sister held herself that screamed *Vogue*. I simultaneously admired and hated her for it.

Cecelia arrived home one afternoon having heard about a local competition called Model Quest. There was to be an evening wear parade and a casual dress section as well as some catwalking. The winner would go on to represent our local area in the regional finals, and so on and so forth, with the final prize including a professional modelling contract.

'I'm doing it,' my sister said, as she set the dinner table that evening.

'I don't know,' Mum said thoughtfully. She turned to face my sister. 'We'll see. I'll have to talk to Dad about it.'

Lying in bed that night, the strains of my parents' discussion wafted down the hallway.

'I don't think it's such a *terrible* idea,' said my mother.

'It's not going to end well,' cautioned my father.

'She wants to have a go at it.' My mother was clearly coming around to the idea. 'This is something she *really* wants to do, Bordy.'

'I'm not coming to watch. I don't want any part of it.'

My father always wanted us to excel academically. Sport was a worthy extracurricular activity, or perhaps music, but this, this was a whole different, dangerous kettle of fish.

'Okay.' A slight hesitance crept into my mother's voice.

My father was sullen the evening Cecelia and Mum pulled out of the driveway on the way to Model Quest. The silver-and-purple floor-length dress my mother had made my sister for her grade ten formal was in a suit bag, draped over the back seat. My sister's duffel bag of ironed and folded clothes for the casual wear section sat on the seat behind her.

At home, Bronson, Dad and I ate the cottage cheese and bacon pasta Mum had left for our dinner. I passed some time watching *Degrassi Junior High*; Lucy was throwing a secret house party while her parents were out of town. I liked Lucy. She reminded me a bit of my sister. She had the same long, thin torso and limbs, and was just as obsessed with clothes and fashion as Cecelia. Lucy wore sparkly, tight-fitting bodysuits. Giant butterfly clips restrained her long, thick afro hair. Her earrings were always enormous, or mismatched, and she could rock a scarf like Prince.

I was meditating on Lucy's innate hipness when Mum and Cecelia burst through the front door. My sister was holding a small red and gold trophy inscribed with the words *Model Quest, Local Heat Winner*. Dad, who was sitting in his cane armchair listening to music, stared at Cecelia wordlessly. He did not look pleased.

'She won!' my mother said, as if she was exhausted with processing what had just happened and needed to sit down for a moment. 'We have to go back for the regional heats in three weeks.'

'Hmmph,' grunted my father, and he closed his eyes and sat back in his chair to finish listening to his Tracy Chapman record.

———————————————

Month after month, the trophies kept coming. They grew larger and larger as the competition drew on. My sister walked around the house permanently haloed in triumph, and soon the rest of us – everyone except my father – were barracking for her. The national Model Quest finals were to be held at a posh hotel in the city. My father held firm in his disapproval. Mum bought tickets for herself, Bronson and I to attend.

———————

There's a moment, around sixteen or seventeen, when you suddenly see your parents – really *see* them – for who they are: apart, as individual people. You understand aspects of their lives or personalities. Things about them start to make sense. There was always a gulf between my parents. As a twosome, they worked well. But this seemed to be *despite* their differences, and there were indeed many. My father had a great sense of humour, when he was in the mood, but he was mostly serious. When his temper appeared, it flashed suddenly and impulsively. Dad was always the firm hand of discipline: the hand that wielded the black leather slipper that whacked down on our thighs to punish the worst of our transgressions – the slipper we slyly hid, when we knew we'd done something worthy of his rage. When Dad was angry, the veins in his forehead would bulge, his eyes became deep pits of fire.

My mother, on the other hand, was mostly relaxed and level-headed. You had to really go out of your way to push her buttons. She was creative; good with people; patient. My father saw things in polarities, while my mother operated on the full spectrum.

In my early teens, while riffling through a stack of dusty cobwebbed boxes in our garage, I'd stumbled upon a scrapbook. It was thin, unassuming, the kind a primary school child might buy to complete a school project. Carefully pasted into its pages were newspaper clippings: reviews of London stage plays my mother had appeared in; write-ups about English soap operas in which she'd played small parts. I'd carefully brushed the dust from the cover and brought the scrapbook out of the garage and into the house.

'Why did you stop acting?' I'd asked. 'Why didn't you go back to it?'

I'd seen her in productions at the New Theatre, in Newtown, and in a few more local plays, but these clippings were from serious performances. *Career* performances. This was Big Time.

'Well . . .' Mum had paused for a moment, as if unsure how to explain it. 'I guess I . . . got married, and then we came to Australia. I did start working professionally. Remember that play you came to see at the Ensemble Theatre? You were all quite little. We had chickens onstage, and the night you came to see the play they escaped?' Mum laughed in recollection. 'It did really well, actually, that play. The director got funding for us to go and do a full season in Fiji. It was a big deal. I wanted to go, but I couldn't because I had young children.' She paused, sighed. 'It wasn't the *responsible* thing to do. The tour was cancelled because of me. I wasn't offered work again professionally after that.'

'Someone else could have looked after us for a week!' I said, incredulously, thinking of all the neighbourhood kids my mum had cared for on various occasions, of my father's relatively flexible teaching job.

'I know.' Silence had hung in the air between us, and I'd understood.

Now I sat between my brother and my mother, under the gleaming crystal chandeliers of the hotel. The girls on stage – young women, really – swung their waif-thin hips down the catwalk, jutting out the places where their curves should be.

Their long, straight hair hung down past their shoulder blades, brushed to a *Cleo* cover-shoot shine.

Then there was Cecelia: full-lipped and high-bottomed, long brown legs striding confidently beneath the short sunflower yellow dress my mother had managed to buy after squirrelling away bits and pieces from the housekeeping money my father gave her. Layers of black tulle made the skirt stiff so that it stood out from her hips, like a tutu. Cecelia was a spunky black-magic pixie, sparkling and vibrant. Her hair was cornrow braided flat to her head with the long ends hanging down her back. She was beautiful, my sister. *Breathtaking.* Not despite her blackness, but inextricably entwined with it. I sat up straighter in my chair to watch as she glided around the stage, flashing her wide, perfect smile. This was why she'd come this far – the *only* way she'd come this far. She was *so* much more stunning than everyone else on the stage. *Indisputably.* Everyone's eyes were glued to her. I felt my entire body swelling with pride.

We waited patiently while the judges tallied the results. We watched as two plain-looking white girls were awarded runner-up and first place. The winners walked up to collect their modelling contract prizes. I understood. I *understood.* My sister's kind of beauty, it wasn't considered neutral. It wasn't *blank canvas* beauty, but I knew, and everyone else in the whole room knew, she had won. *We* had won. I wished my father had been there to see it.

24.

UN-BECOMING YOURSELF. SLIPPING on another skin. Masking the truth. Playing at other realities. I'd always been attracted to the artifice of acting. It seemed similar to reading to me, to writing even, in a way. Some magic kind of thing. I could try on other lives, pretend I wasn't me. I'd always had a chorus role in my high school musicals, right from grade seven, but in grade eleven, I decided it was time to shoot for a main part.

This is how it happened, that folklore way of spinning a tale.

I stood in the lounge room, digging my hands into a mini-packet of Coles popcorn.

'Those snacks are supposed to be for school!' Mum scolded as she came in the back door with a basket of washing.

'Sorry.' I licked my salt-covered fingers. 'We're doing *Twelfth Night* as the school play this year instead of a musical,' I announced. 'I'm going to audition for a main part, I think.'

'*Twelfth Night!*' Mum echoed enthusiastically. She put on her mock *I am acting* face. 'I left no ring with her!' She strode purposefully across the lounge room and scratched her head theatrically

242

as she delivered the line. 'What *means* this lady? Fortune forbid my outsides did not charm her!' She shook her head forlornly.

'Mum!' I groaned. 'God. That was *awful!*'

'Shut up! Anyway, it's a good play,' she said approvingly. 'I can help you with your audition, if you like. What part are you going for?'

'I want the main role,' I said defiantly. 'I want to play Viola.'

'Have you read the play?' Mum dropped the washing basket down onto the wooden floorboards, sat down on the couch and commenced folding. I sat down next to her and reached for a handful of clothes.

'Yes,' I said indignantly. 'Of course I have.'

'Then you know that Viola has a twin brother, Sebastian.'

'And?'

'Well . . .' Mum paused. 'If you got the role of Viola, who would play Sebastian?'

'Bollocks.' I hadn't thought that far.

Mum picked up a small stack of towels and made for the hallway cupboard.

'I'm going to read Viola's monologue for the audition anyway,' I said stubbornly, 'and just see what happens.'

'Fair enough. You never know, they might give you the part and make one of the other kids go blackface to play Sebastian. After all, it's supposed to be a comedy.'

I looked over at her. She pulled her head out of the linen cupboard and smirked at me mischievously. We both collapsed with giggles.

'That's not even funny,' I said. 'I bet they would.'

I arrived early at school the day the cast list was to be pinned up on the drama block noticeboard. Standing at the back of the small cluster of eager thespians, I felt butterflies flapping around in my stomach. I was nervous. I *really* wanted this. My drama teacher, Miss Silverstein, was the director. I knew she would be fair in her casting decisions, and I knew my audition had been good.

I ran my eye over the sheet of A4 paper tacked into place high at the top of the noticeboard with shiny gold drawing pins. There it was, on line three:

Maxine Clarke . . . . *Countess Olivia*

I moved away from the throng of excited hopefuls, smiling at the shouts of congratulations. Once over to the side of the drama crowd, I fished my copy of the book out of my bag. *The Countess Olivia*, the character description read, *a beautiful Illyrian lady of noble birth*. I remembered her now. Olivia was a main role. Not as many lines as Viola, but a main role nonetheless. Olivia was the standoffish and beautiful countess with whom Duke Orsino was in mad, feverish and unrequited love. She was an ice-queen heartbreaker, unattainable. I hadn't paid her character much mind at all when I read the script. On a subconscious level, I'd just assumed it wasn't realistic for me to audition for the part.

This is how we see ourselves.

This is how we're crushed.

The bell rang. As I walked towards homeroom, I thought about how I might play Olivia. I thought about Cecelia, and the way she'd strode haughtily around that catwalk with her head held high. I knew precisely what my Olivia would be like. I could feel her coming to life inside my body: waking.

'Fuck!' Selina said, when I gave her the news in our first lesson of the day.

'*I know.*' I thought about the roles I'd seen my mother play on Australian stages over the years: Tituba, the Bar-Bajan maid in *The Crucible*; Calpurnia, the black housekeeper in the stage adaptation of *To Kill a Mockingbird*. Now I was Countess Olivia. It was only a high school production, but this was *huge*. I sat next to Selina, both of us digesting the development in stunned silence.

Mum had always worked various part-time jobs around us kids, but with my brother and I now at high school, and my sister at university, she'd gone back into permanent employment in an administrative role.

'Hello, is Cleopatra Clarke there, please?' I called her the moment I got home, trying to sound businesslike, so her boss wouldn't know her kid was calling her on work time. 'They cast me as Olivia!' I yelled, as soon as I heard her voice.

'*Olivia?*' she said. Then: 'Oh my god! Congratulations. THEY MADE YOU OLIVIA!' Her voice was laced with excitement and disbelief.

After Bronson and I had cleared away the dinner plates that evening, I handed Mum the costuming note.

'A long black dress and a black veil,' she said. 'Well, I'm not buying a whole new outfit just for the play. You can wear that black empire line dress you already have, and I'll get some lace from Spotlight to make a veil.'

'It says a white dress, too.' I pointed towards the bottom of the note. 'For the wedding scene with Sebastian at the end.'

Mum stared at the note. 'Come here,' she said. She led me across the lounge room to her bedroom. There, she opened the mirrored built-in wardrobe, took out a garment bag and lay it flat on her bed.

'Open it.'

I slowly pulled the zipper all the way down to reveal a long ivory dress with thin spaghetti straps. Layer upon layer of lace cascaded down the dress in horizontal rings. I wasn't really one for dresses, but this gown was breathtaking.

'There's your dress for the wedding scene!' Mum said triumphantly. 'Try it on!'

'Where'd you get this from?!' I wriggled out of my school skirt and stepped into the dress, pulling it up over my t-shirt. It fit perfectly; it was vintage-looking, but somehow modern at the same time. It was exquisite. It seemed like it had been made especially for me – for this exact moment and purpose.

'It was floor-length on me,' Mum said, 'but it actually looks beautiful a bit shorter as well.'

'I've never seen you in it!'

'Oh, I made it about twenty years ago. It took me *forever*. It was my wedding dress.'

I smoothed my hands over the lace, and stared at myself in the mirror. My long black braids hung down over my shoulders. My skin was almost clear now. You could see my cheekbones a bit more, without the grey-black marks which had plagued my face. My lips were full; my eyebrows were dark and defined. My arms and legs were slim and shapely underneath the gown.

'You look beautiful,' my mother said softly. 'Just beautiful.'

When Mum had worn the dress some twenty years earlier, she'd been the talk of black Tottenham: Millie and Robert

Critchlow's middle daughter, Cleopatra, the young Guyanese actress who'd newly graduated from the National School of Speech and Drama. A beauty – and my father had somehow nabbed her. My father, Bordeaux Mathias Nathanial Clarke, the firstborn son of two Jamaicans, named with all the pomp and expectation that entailed. At twenty-five, Mum had married one of the first men in her community to secure a degree from a British university: my father with his soundwaves, and equations, and geek-glasses. Her sweetheart, with his numbers and his slightly abrasive ways.

Standing in my parents' room, in my mother's wedding dress, my mind conjured the old photographs of my parents: the ones yellowing with age in our family albums, on the almost-buckling shelves in the next room. My father, in flared cords and tight-fitting shirts, his oval-shaped afro rising high above his head. My drama–school–graduate mother, dainty and petite in velour turtlenecks and large wooden earrings, sparkly eyed and beautiful. Both of them Black Britain to a tee: full-to-bursting with seventies hippie hopefulness. And, my god, their *youth*.

———————————

Dad had this *list* of things. Things that needed doing around the house. Things he needed to fix. He was fiercely determined to get all of them sorted by the end of the weekend. I sat in the lounge room, sunk into the beige settee, watching him mend the hole in the back screen door over the top of my Judy Blume book. Dad stopped suddenly, looked over at me.

'Let me tell you something.' He beckoned me over, like he had something really important he wanted to share. Something that couldn't possibly wait.

I put down the book and moved to stand dutifully behind him. He pushed the sheet of flyscreen down inside the door fitting, his eyes fixed on his work as he spoke. 'You will have to work harder than them all,' he said. 'Because you're a *black girl*. If you want what they have, to be deemed as good as them, you'll have to work ten times as hard. I'm telling you that now. You remember it. Whatever you want to do, do it ten times better. *Then* they'll see you on their level.' Dad pushed his thick glasses up his nose, bent, and continued slotting the new mesh into the metal frame of the sliding door, grunting to signal that our chat was over.

I walked slowly back to my book, glancing back at him every now and then. I was perplexed. I wasn't sure if he had actually looked up, gestured me over and counselled me, or if I'd just somehow imagined it. He was behaving as if our conversation hadn't even happened. I shrugged it off. Sometimes my dad just came out with random strange things like that.

———————

The following Monday was hot. That can't-get-away-from-it late February heat. A lazy even-the-flies-seem-slower humidity hung in the air. I caught the early bus home from school, desperate to get home to the air conditioning as quickly as possible. I rounded the corner into Hectare Street, the back of my school shirt sticking uncomfortably to my back underneath my schoolbag. Two women across the street – elderly neighbours of ours – were chatting over their front fences, looking towards our house. I smiled over at them. One of them half-heartedly raised her hand. The other smiled, but it somehow seemed more like a grimace. I climbed the front steps of our house, put the key in the lock. For some odd reason, I turned and looked across the street again. My neighbours were still staring at me. They quickly turned away.

I closed the door behind me. Our lounge room looked different. It took me a few moments to realise why. The stereo speakers were gone: the two enormous hulking bass-beating beauties Dad had tinkered with for the past ten years. My backpack slid off my shoulder and onto the lounge room floor. We'd been robbed! As I ran for the phone to call my mother, I noticed the glaring white wall space where the shelving should have been. Dad's meticulously catalogued records – in their hundreds – had disappeared. There was a note taped to the wall. I reached for it.

Dear kids, it said, in Dad's neat cursive handwriting. *Don't worry about the stereo: I have taken it.*

What did he mean he had *taken it*? *Where* had he taken it? What had happened to my dad? I was confused – and terrified.

I went to the kitchen and dialled Mum's work number.

'The stereo's gone,' I told her. 'And all of Dad's records. And there's a note.' I read it out to her.

Mum went quiet at the other end of the line for at least ten seconds. 'Can you . . . can you . . . can you please check his side of the wardrobe?' she asked softly. 'And see if his clothes are in there?'

I rushed to the wardrobe. Dad's shoes, jackets, clothes, ties – everything was gone. His whole side of the wardrobe was bare.

'There's . . . there's *nothing there*,' I confirmed. 'He left a letter for you on the bed.'

'I'm coming home,' Mum said. She sounded far away, muffled. 'I'm leaving right now. I'll be there in half an hour.'

I could hear Bronson leaping up the front steps. He was in his second year at the local state selective high school, and his bus arrived at the corner of our street about ten minutes after the early bus from my school.

'What's going on?' My brother looked at me standing in the centre of the lounge room with the note in my hands.

'Um . . .' I stumbled, wondering how to explain. 'Dad's gone.'

'What do you mean, he's *gone*?'

I showed him the note. Bronson looked around the half-empty room.

'His clothes aren't in the wardrobe. I called Mum. She's on her way home.'

My brother's eyes widened.

There were so many things I thought about in that half hour, waiting for Mum to come home. I thought about the two ladies across the street, and how they must've watched my father going back and forth, in and out of our house, carting his belongings. I thought about how, in his usual socially dysfunctional way, Dad had broadcast his departure to the entire neighbourhood even before telling his kids or his wife. I thought about the note; wondered whether he'd known I'd be the first one home; whether he'd planned it that way. If he knew I'd have to explain his disappearance to Bronson. If he'd thought about me phoning my mother at work to deliver the news that her husband had left. I wondered whether he'd deliberately waited until Cecelia was away for a few nights at her university camp, to shield her.

———

There was a woman – that much soon became clear. There had been another woman, unbeknown to anyone, for years. The evening squash games. The missed school debates. Bringing cheesecake home every Wednesday night. Our minds wandered with cruel possibilities.

Mum picked herself up, held it together, got on with business. Money was tight. Tensions ran high. Some weekends, my father inexplicably came back around to our house and mowed the lawn. We would watch him through the window as he sweated up and down the nature strip. Then he'd come into the house, shower, and leave again.

Several months after he moved out, Dad turned up on the doorstep to mow the lawn, moved to open the front door, and found the locks had been changed. I watched through the lounge room window as he stood on the front steps, smouldering with rage.

The whole of Kellyville village heard what had happened between Bordeaux and Cleopatra Clarke, between the young black couple who'd purchased the little blonde-brick house on Hectare Street, next to old Betty and Jack's place. The whole village remembered when they had first arrived: him mowing the lawn of a Saturday morning, thick glasses fogged up with perspiration, black muscles shining from underneath his dark blue Bonds singlet, striped terry-towelling sweatband circling his afro. They remembered scratching their heads, staring over their fences; the gossip that had spread. They remembered the home Bordeaux and Cleopatra had made: the home most of them had been in and out of at various times, packed with playdough, and laughter, and love.

Every second Saturday morning, my father picked us up and drove us out to Ryde, where he shared a place with the woman he'd been secretly seeing for several years. We would be invited just for the day; he would drop us back home in the afternoon. Dad's new partner was softly spoken and demure. She had shoulder-length blonde hair and vague green eyes, and wore long flowing skirts that brushed against her calves. Dad's new partner wasn't a patch on my mum.

There are myriad ways I've heard it told. The young black wunderkind: the son of a cane-cutter, with the god-knew-how-it-happened first-class degree in pure mathematics. Gough Whitlam, the sensible new Australian prime minister and his dismantling of the last vestiges of the White Australia Policy. That fool English politician Enoch Powell, and his *rivers of blood* anti-immigration nonsense. Two academics arranging to meet at London's Victoria station. A Qantas jumbo jet, and my parents' unforgettable arrival in Sydney, in 1976, at the Man Friday Hotel.

This is how it happened, or else what's a story for.

EPILOGUE

IT'S THE END of my son's first school holidays. He's excited to go back to his primary school. He got up early this morning, found his uniform, and was dressed in his little green Stubbies shorts and bright yellow collared shirt way before his baby sister and I even woke up. My son can't wait to return to his ABCs, to junior choir practice, to rehearsing his class assembly item and swimming lessons at the local pool.

I'm walking slowly along behind him as he skips ahead: through the park just across the road from our flat; past the piano shop which never seems to have any customers in it.

'Come on, Mama! Come on!' He presses the button for the pedestrian crossing.

We make our way across to the other side of North Road, my little daughter bouncing contentedly in the makeshift stretchy baby sling knotted across my front, peeping curiously out at the busy peak hour traffic.

'Slow down, darling.'

'Mama!' My son suddenly stops short. 'I had a sip from my drink bottle when I was at home, and I left it in the lounge room!' He pauses on the footpath; swings his green standard-issue school backpack down onto the concrete. We both look down. The mesh drink-bottle holder on the side of his bag is empty.

'Well, I guess we'd better go back and get it, darling.'

He looks up at me, his little face starting to crumple. 'I don't want to be late, Mama! It's the first day back.' His chin trembles against the strap of the dark green sunhat wedged tightly on his head.

'Okay . . . okay. There's a service station coming up. Let's just duck in and get you a bottle of water there.'

'Thank you, Mama.' Crisis averted, my son picks up his bag and slings it back onto his shoulders.

The pop-candy luminescence of the petrol station is difficult to process on so little sleep. The baby is teething and kept me up all night, with her forlorn wails of agony.

'Just the water?'

'Yes, thanks.'

The woman behind the counter has just started her shift for the morning. She pins on her nametag and pulls her hair back into a quick ponytail. She scans the bottle of water, returns it to me. 'That'll be two dollars, thanks.'

I scratch around in my jeans pocket for the right coin.

'Aw . . .' The shop attendant takes the money and wriggles around the counter to where we're standing. She leans in close and looks down into my sling. My daughter's eyes have finally been lulled shut by the movement and warmth of my body.

'She's *sooo* adorable!' the attendant coos. She walks around me in a circle, looking at the stretchy piece of material knotted at my back and wound over both my shoulders. 'It's amazing, how you people carry your babies. It just seems to be, like, *instinctive!*'

254

You people. Suddenly, there's that chest-tightening feeling. That heart-in-my-throat, pulse-in-my-temples fear. The dry tongue. The gasping for breath. The remembering how it can happen anywhere, at any time. That can't-think freeze. I am four years old, on my first day of preschool, standing underneath the mulberry tree watching Carlita Allen's lip curl up with disgust as she stares at me. I am slouched down on the high school bus, head bowed, pretending not to notice the whispered name-calling. I take a deep breath in, smile, and hustle my son out of the petrol station.

We turn the corner, walking past modest family houses on well-established blocks. We skirt around the large grey four-wheel drives parked in the streets surrounding the school.

My son runs inside the school gate. 'Can I go and play now? Some of my friends are over there.'

I tighten my grip on his hand.

'Mama! Let go of me! I want to go and play!'

I reach down and give my son a hug. 'You have a good day, darling.'

On the way home, I stop in the park across the road from our flat. My daughter has woken up. I untie the sling, lay the long stretch of fabric on the grass and sit my daughter on it. I lie down next to her, on my back, on the damp buffalo grass, and gaze up at the tall paperbark trees, their branches rustling in the summer breeze. I turn my head to look over at my daughter. She has shuffled over to the edge of the makeshift play mat and is busy shoving slyly collected fistfuls of dirt into her mouth.

This is my children's country, of that I am sure. They were born here, in this beautiful, wide, brown, scorched and stolen land. My children's early ancestors were part of the Atlantic slave trade. They were dragged screaming from their homes in West Africa and chained by their necks and ankles, deep in the mouldy hulls of slave ships – destined to become free labour for the New World. If slaves were lucky, they died in transit to the Caribbean – bodies thrown overboard, washed clean of the blood, sweat and faeces in which they'd spent most of the harrowing journey. If they survived, they found themselves mid-nightmare: put to work on the harshest plantations on earth, at the hands of some of the cruellest masters in the history of the Atlantic slave trade.

My children are the descendants of those unbroken.

ACKNOWLEDGEMENTS

I LOVE THIS country. I love this country, but I believe we could be so much kinder to each other. So much more equitable. So much better. I hope I live to see it happen. I wrote this book because I believe stories like these need to be written into Australian letters. Stories like mine need to be heard, and seen, both by those outside of them and those with similar tales. I wanted to show the lasting impact of living in a brown body in Australia in the eighties and nineties on one child. I wanted to show the extreme toll that casual, overt and institutionalised racism can take: the way it erodes us all. Sadly, there were many, many more stories which could have gone into this book. Choosing was a difficult process indeed.

One of my favourite poets, Nikki Giovanni, wrote a poem called 'Nikki-Rosa' in which she lists the trials of growing up in a poor, black household. At the end of the poem, she says something like: *people will never understand that all the time, I was quite happy.* This memoir is about a very specific aspect of my childhood: interactions and misunderstandings around race and ethnicity. I consider myself to have had a privileged upbringing in so many other ways. There was always food on our table, love and joy in our home. I am ever grateful to my parents for the extraordinary job they did, under what, at times, must have been incredibly trying circumstances.

Some events in this book have been slightly condensed in time, for the sake of narrative arc, as is sometimes necessary in creative non-fiction. All names other than mine have also been changed: poets can't afford lawsuits. To the significant people in my life who do not appear in this book, know that I love you nevertheless – and know that that's a *great* thing!

Thank you, first and foremost, to my family: 'Bronson', 'Cecelia', 'Cleopatra' and 'Bordeaux', and my beloved son and daughter. Thank you 'Selina' for always being by my side. Thank you to those teachers who were a guiding light: most notably Annie F., Madeleine S. and Ian B. I apologise *unreservedly* for the Great Tribal Dancing Hoax, and I hope that you'll forgive me. 'Bhagita', I'm sorry. I will carry both the shame, and the lesson, of what I did for eternity.

In 2013, I received the Hazel Rowley Fellowship for Biography to research my family history. The trip this extraordinary fellowship funded assisted me in the writing of *The Hate Race*, and also allowed me to commence research for a planned follow-up book. I'm so very proud to be a small part of Hazel's legacy.

In 2013, I also received funding from the Literature Board of the Australia Council for the Arts, which assisted me in completing an early draft of *The Hate Race*. For this, I am similarly grateful.

My first-ever reading from an early manuscript of *The Hate Race* took place in 2014, in the foyer workshop space of the Ren i Tang hotel in Penang, Malaysia, as part of the inaugural WrICE writing residency. Thank you to Francesca Rendle-Short,

David Carlin, Melissa Lucashenko and all of the writers who took part in the residency for providing a safe, friendly, enthusiastic space in which to slowly unfurl my ideas.

Dave Eggers. Thank you for your early reading of *The Hate Race*, and for that *just keep going* message that arrived to rescue me at the most existential of times.

Thank you to Hachette: who didn't baulk (no, not *even* at the title). Thank you in particular to Anna Egelstaff, Ali Lavau, Kate Stevens, Fiona Hazard, Justin Ractliffe, Louise Sherwin-Stark, Christopher Sims, Mary Bayley and the always-there-in-spirit Matt Richell, who is very much a part of this book's journey. Thank you to Tara Wynne at Curtis Brown, Susan Armstrong at Conville and Walsh, and Sarah Castleton and the team at Corsair.

Allison Colpoys. This is the third cover you've designed for me. You are a genius. A *genius*. It's an absolute pleasure and honour to have my covers designed by you. Thanks for always *getting it*.

Last, but not least, thank you to my publisher, Robert Watkins. From the moment we met, I couldn't imagine putting this book out into the world without you at the helm, and now here we are. Shit. *Here we are.*

This book is dedicated to the children of Australia, including mine. May all your classrooms and playgrounds be kept safe.

Room to Read®

About Maxine Beneba Clarke and Room to Read

Maxine Beneba Clarke is a committed writer ambassador for Room to Read, an innovative global non-profit which seeks to transform the lives of millions of children in ten developing countries through its holistic Literacy and Girls' Education programs.

Working in collaboration with local communities, partner organisations and governments, Room to Read focuses its efforts on developing reading skills in primary school-aged children because literacy is the foundation for all future learning. Since it was founded in 2000, Room to Read has impacted the lives of over 10 million children by establishing school libraries, publishing original children's books in more than 25 local languages, constructing child-friendly classrooms and supporting educators with training and resources to teach reading, writing and active listening.

Room to Read is changing children's lives in Bangladesh, Cambodia, India, Laos, Nepal, South Africa, Sri Lanka, Tanzania, Vietnam and Zambia.

As Maxine says, 'I support Room to Read because education and imagination open worlds, bring opportunity, and change lives. Every child on earth deserves access to education, and in an inequitable world, it is organisations like Room to Read which fight for the forgotten.'

For more information, www.roomtoread.org.

Maxine Beneba Clarke is a widely published Australian writer of Afro-Caribbean descent and the author of the poetry collections *Gil Scott Heron Is on Parole* and *Nothing Here Needs Fixing*. Maxine's short fiction, non-fiction and poetry have been published in numerous publications including *Overland*, *The Age*, *Meanjin*, *The Saturday Paper* and *The Big Issue*. Her critically acclaimed short fiction collection *Foreign Soil* (2014) won the ABIA for Literary Fiction Book of the Year 2015, the 2015 Indie Book Award for Debut Fiction, and Maxine was also named as one of the *Sydney Morning Herald*'s Best Young Novelists for 2015, as well as being shortlisted for the Matt Richell Award for New Writing at the 2015 ABIAs and the 2015 Stella Prize.